# DUTIES AND BLESSINGS OF THE PRIESTHOOD

## Basic Manual for Priesthood Holders, Part A

Published by
The Church of Jesus Christ of Latter-day Saints
Salt Lake City, Utah
Revised 2000

## Comments and Suggestions

Your comments and suggestions about this manual would be appreciated. Please submit them to:

Curriculum Planning
50 East North Temple Street, Floor 24
Salt Lake City, UT 84150-3200
USA
E-mail: cur-development@ldschurch.org

Please list your name, address, ward, and stake. Be sure to give the title of the manual. Then offer your comments and suggestions about the manual's strengths and areas of potential improvement.

# CONTENTS

# Contents

# INTRODUCTION

## Using This Manual

This manual provides 35 lessons related to basic gospel principles and the responsibilities of Aaronic Priesthood and Melchizedek Priesthood bearers. As prompted by the Spirit, leaders and teachers should plan and teach lessons that address the spiritual, emotional, and temporal needs of the members in their branch or ward.

This manual should be used as the instruction manual for both the Melchizedek Priesthood and Aaronic Priesthood in units of the Church where *Teachings of Presidents of the Church* and Aaronic Priesthood manuals are not yet published in the needed language. In such units, copies of this manual should be made available to all holders of the Melchizedek Priesthood and to Aaronic Priesthood leaders and instructors. Local leaders should consult *Information for Priesthood and Auxiliary Leaders on Curriculum* for the schedule showing which years part A and part B of *Duties and Blessings of the Priesthood* are to be used.

In units of the Church where *Teachings of Presidents of the Church* and Aaronic Priesthood manuals are available, this manual should be used (1) as a resource for Melchizedek Priesthood instruction on first and fourth Sundays; (2) as a supplementary resource for Aaronic Priesthood instruction; and (3) as designated, for Relief Society "Teachings for Our Time" lessons on fourth Sundays. In such units, copies of the manual should be made available to the leaders and instructors in the Relief Society, Melchizedek Priesthood, and Aaronic Priesthood. In addition, leaders may encourage Melchizedek Priesthood holders to purchase a copy of this manual for personal study and for family teaching in the home.

## Preparing to Teach

Teaching helps provided in this manual include a "Teacher Preparation" section, questions teachers could ask, suggestions for class participation, and directions for using pictures and charts. In addition to the discussion questions and methods suggested, teachers may choose to use other methods or lesson approaches they find effective to involve their class members and stimulate participation and learning. Almost every lesson suggests the use of a chalkboard, so if possible teachers should arrange to have a chalkboard and chalk available for each lesson. Many of the visual aids suggested for use as posters could be drawn or written on the chalkboard. Other suggestions for teaching can be found in the *Teaching Guidebook* (34595) and in *Teaching, No Greater Call* (36123).

Class members should be encouraged to prepare for class discussion by studying the assigned lesson during the week. They should also be encouraged to bring their scriptures.

**Involving Members with Disabilities**

During His mortal ministry, Jesus went up into the mountain near the Sea of Galilee.

"And great multitudes came unto him, having with them those that were lame, blind, dumb, maimed, and many others, and cast them down at Jesus' feet; and he healed them:

"Insomuch that the multitude wondered, when they saw the dumb to speak, the maimed to be whole, the lame to walk, and the blind to see: and they glorified the God of Israel" (Matthew 15:30–31).

The Savior set the example for us in feeling compassion for those with disabilities. When He visited the Nephites after His Resurrection, He said:

"Behold, my bowels are filled with compassion towards you.

"Have ye any that are sick among you? Bring them hither. Have ye any that are lame, or blind, or halt, or maimed, or leprous, or that are withered, or that are deaf, or that are afflicted in any manner? Bring them hither and I will heal them, for I have compassion upon you; my bowels are filled with mercy" (3 Nephi 17:6–7).

As a teacher in a Church classroom, you are in an excellent position to show compassion. Although not usually trained to give professional assistance to class members with disabilities, teachers should desire to understand and include these members in the learning activities of the class. Class members with mental, physical, emotional, and other disabilities may need special attention. The following guidelines should help you reach every member:

- Strive to understand the needs and abilities of each class member.

- Check in advance with a class member before calling on him to read, pray, or otherwise participate. Ask such questions as "How do you feel about reading in class?" or "Would you feel comfortable praying in class?" If appropriate, check with priesthood leaders, parents, and family members to determine the member's special needs.

- Try to increase and improve the involvement and learning of the member with a disability.

- Ensure that each class member treats every other class member with respect.

- Be natural, friendly, and warm. Every son of God needs love and understanding.

As a teacher in the Church, remember that each member, regardless of physical, mental, emotional, or social capacity, has the potential for growth toward exaltation. You have an obligation to help each individual learn gospel principles in your class. Remember the words of the Savior: "Inasmuch as ye have done it unto one of the least of these my brethren, ye have done it unto me" (Matthew 25:40).

# THE LIVING CHRIST

## THE TESTIMONY OF THE APOSTLES

### THE CHURCH OF JESUS CHRIST OF LATTER-DAY SAINTS

As we commemorate the birth of Jesus Christ two millennia ago, we offer our testimony of the reality of His matchless life and the infinite virtue of His great atoning sacrifice. None other has had so profound an influence upon all who have lived and will yet live upon the earth.

He was the Great Jehovah of the Old Testament, the Messiah of the New. Under the direction of His Father, He was the creator of the earth. "All things were made by him; and without him was not any thing made that was made" (John 1:3). Though sinless, He was baptized to fulfill all righteousness. He "went about doing good" (Acts 10:38), yet was despised for it. His gospel was a message of peace and goodwill. He entreated all to follow His example. He walked the roads of Palestine, healing the sick, causing the blind to see, and raising the dead. He taught the truths of eternity, the reality of our premortal existence, the purpose of our life on earth, and the potential for the sons and daughters of God in the life to come.

He instituted the sacrament as a reminder of His great atoning sacrifice. He was arrested and condemned on spurious charges, convicted to satisfy a mob, and sentenced to die on Calvary's cross. He gave His life to atone for the sins of all mankind. His was a great vicarious gift in behalf of all who would ever live upon the earth.

We solemnly testify that His life, which is central to all human history, neither began in Bethlehem nor concluded on Calvary. He was the Firstborn of the Father, the Only Begotten Son in the flesh, the Redeemer of the world.

He rose from the grave to "become the firstfruits of them that slept" (1 Corinthians 15:20). As Risen Lord, He visited among those He had loved in life. He also ministered among His "other sheep" (John 10:16) in ancient America. In the modern world, He and His Father appeared to the boy Joseph Smith, ushering in the long-promised "dispensation of the fulness of times" (Ephesians 1:10).

Of the Living Christ, the Prophet Joseph wrote: "His eyes were as a flame of fire; the hair of his head was white like the pure snow; his countenance shone above the brightness of the sun; and his voice was as the sound of the rushing of great waters, even the voice of Jehovah, saying:

"I am the first and the last; I am he who liveth, I am he who was slain; I am your advocate with the Father" (D&C 110:3–4).

Of Him the Prophet also declared: "And now, after the many testimonies which have been given of him, this is the testimony, last of all, which we give of him: That he lives!

"For we saw him, even on the right hand of God; and we heard the voice bearing record that he is the Only Begotten of the Father—

"That by him, and through him, and of him, the worlds are and were created, and the inhabitants thereof are begotten sons and daughters unto God" (D&C 76:22–24).

We declare in words of solemnity that His priesthood and His Church have been restored upon the earth—"built upon the foundation of . . . apostles and prophets, Jesus Christ himself being the chief corner stone" (Ephesians 2:20).

We testify that He will someday return to earth. "And the glory of the Lord shall be revealed, and all flesh shall see it together" (Isaiah 40:5). He will rule as King of Kings and reign as Lord of Lords, and every knee shall bend and every tongue shall speak in worship before Him. Each of us will stand to be judged of Him according to our works and the desires of our hearts.

We bear testimony, as His duly ordained Apostles—that Jesus is the Living Christ, the immortal Son of God. He is the great King Immanuel, who stands today on the right hand of His Father. He is the light, the life, and the hope of the world. His way is the path that leads to happiness in this life and eternal life in the world to come. God be thanked for the matchless gift of His divine Son.

THE FIRST PRESIDENCY

*Gordon B. Hinckley*
*Thomas S. Monson*
*James E. Faust*

THE QUORUM OF THE TWELVE

*Boyd K. Packer*
*L. Tom Perry*
*David B. Haight*
*Neal A. Maxwell*
*Russell M. Nelson*
*Dallin H. Oaks*

*M. Russell Ballard*
*Joseph B. Wirthlin*
*Richard G. Scott*
*Robert D. Hales*
*Jeffrey R. Holland*
*Henry B. Eyring*

January 1, 2000

# A PROCLAMATION TO THE WORLD

The First Presidency and Council of the Twelve Apostles
of The Church of Jesus Christ of Latter-day Saints

WE, THE FIRST PRESIDENCY and the Council of the Twelve Apostles of The Church of Jesus Christ of Latter-day Saints, solemnly proclaim that marriage between a man and a woman is ordained of God and that the family is central to the Creator's plan for the eternal destiny of His children.

ALL HUMAN BEINGS—male and female—are created in the image of God. Each is a beloved spirit son or daughter of heavenly parents, and, as such, each has a divine nature and destiny. Gender is an essential characteristic of individual pre-mortal, mortal, and eternal identity and purpose.

IN THE PREMORTAL REALM, spirit sons and daughters knew and worshiped God as their Eternal Father and accepted His plan by which His children could obtain a physical body and gain earthly experience to progress toward perfection and ultimately realize his or her divine destiny as an heir of eternal life. The divine plan of happiness enables family relationships to be perpetuated beyond the grave. Sacred ordinances and covenants available in holy temples make it possible for individuals to return to the presence of God and for families to be united eternally.

THE FIRST COMMANDMENT that God gave to Adam and Eve pertained to their potential for parenthood as husband and wife. We declare that God's commandment for His children to multiply and replenish the earth remains in force. We further declare that God has com-manded that the sacred powers of procreation are to be employed only between man and woman, lawfully wedded as husband and wife.

WE DECLARE the means by which mortal life is created to be divinely appointed. We affirm the sanctity of life and of its importance in God's eternal plan.

HUSBAND AND WIFE have a solemn responsibility to love and care for each other and for their children. "Children are an heritage of the Lord" (Psalms 127:3). Parents have a sacred duty to rear their children in love and righteousness, to provide for their physical and spiritual needs, to teach them to love and serve one another, to observe the commandments of God and to be law-abiding citizens wherever they live. Husbands and wives—mothers and fathers—will be held accountable before God for the discharge of these obligations.

THE FAMILY is ordained of God. Marriage between man and woman is essential to His eternal plan. Children are entitled to birth within the bonds of matrimony, and to be reared by a father and a mother who honor marital vows with complete fidelity. Happiness in family life is most likely to be achieved when founded upon the teachings of the Lord Jesus Christ. Successful marriages and families are established and maintained on principles of faith, prayer, repentance, forgiveness, respect, love, compassion, work, and wholesome recreational activities. By divine design, fathers are to preside over their families in love and righteousness and are responsible to provide the necessities of life and protection for their families. Mothers are primarily responsible for the nurture of their children. In these sacred responsibilities, fathers and mothers are obligated to help one another as equal partners. Disability, death, or other circumstances may necessitate individual adaptation. Extended families should lend support when needed.

WE WARN that individuals who violate covenants of chastity, who abuse spouse or offspring, or who fail to fulfill family responsibilities will one day stand accountable before God. Further, we warn that the disintegration of the family will bring upon individuals, communities, and nations the calamities foretold by ancient and modern prophets.

WE CALL UPON responsible citizens and officers of government everywhere to promote those measures designed to maintain and strengthen the family as the fundamental unit of society.

# HISTORY AND ORGANIZATION OF THE PRIESTHOOD

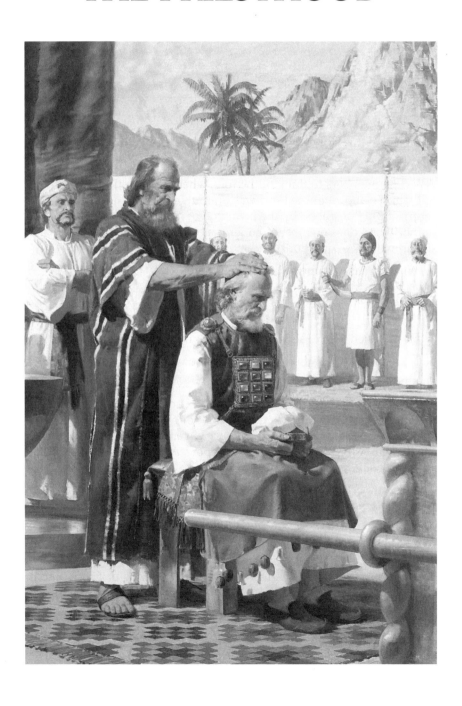

# THE PRIESTHOOD

*Lesson 1*

---

The purpose of this lesson is to help us understand what the priesthood is and how to magnify our callings in the priesthood.

**Introduction**

Ask class members to think of the time when the priesthood was given to them. The Spirit of the Lord was undoubtedly present as they received the priesthood by the laying on of hands from those with authority. As class members ponder that experience, invite them to ask themselves these questions:

1. What actually happened to me that day?

2. Was I a different person after receiving the priesthood?

3. Am I a different person today because I hold the priesthood?

4. Have I been able to serve others through the priesthood?

5. Is my Heavenly Father pleased with the way I use the priesthood?

**The Priesthood Is the Power of God**

"When we [act] in the name of the Lord, as holders of the priesthood, we are doing it in the name and in behalf of our Heavenly Father. Priesthood is the power by which our Heavenly Father works through men" (Harold B. Lee, in Conference Report, Apr. 1973, 128; or *Ensign,* July 1973, 98).

The priesthood is God's eternal power and authority. God accomplishes His work by the priesthood. He created all things by this power, and He governs the earth and heaven by it. We read in the Pearl of Great Price that the priesthood, "which was in the beginning, shall be in the end of the world also" (Moses 6:7).

God and Jesus Christ have given worthy male members of the Church the power of the priesthood so that they can help "to bring to pass the immortality and eternal life of man" (Moses 1:39). The priesthood is the authority of God given to men to act in all things for the salvation of mankind.

Those who hold the priesthood have the authority to act in God's name. Speaking to all priesthood bearers, President Joseph Fielding Smith said:

"We are the Lord's agents; we represent him; he has given us authority which empowers us to do all that is necessary to save and exalt ourselves as well as his other children in the world.

"We are ambassadors of the Lord Jesus Christ. Our commission is to represent him. We are directed . . . to do what he would do if he were personally present" (in Conference Report, Apr. 1971, 47; or *Ensign,* June 1971, 49).

### Priesthood Power Comes through Righteous Living

"All of us who hold the priesthood have the authority to act for the Lord, but the effectiveness of our authority—or if you please, the power that comes through that authority—depends on the pattern of our lives; it depends on our righteousness" (H. Burke Peterson, in Conference Report, Apr. 1976, 50; or *Ensign,* May 1976, 33).

In the Doctrine and Covenants, the Lord has made it clear to us that we must live righteously to have not only the authority, but also the *power* of the priesthood:

"Behold, there are many called, but few are chosen. And why are they not chosen?

"Because their hearts are set so much upon the things of this world, and aspire to the honors of men, that they do not learn this one lesson—

"That the rights of the priesthood are inseparably connected with the powers of heaven, and that the powers of heaven cannot be controlled nor handled only upon the principles of righteousness.

"That they may be conferred upon us, it is true; but when we undertake to cover our sins, or to gratify our pride, our vain ambition, or to exercise control or dominion or compulsion upon the souls of the children of men, in any degree of unrighteousness, behold, the heavens withdraw themselves; the Spirit of the Lord is grieved; and when it is withdrawn, Amen to the priesthood or the authority of that man" (D&C 121:34–37).

- In these verses, the Lord reveals why some priesthood holders are not able to exercise the priesthood with power. Why would these things keep us from having power in the priesthood?

The source of the power of the priesthood is God, who works through the Holy Ghost. To have the Holy Ghost direct us in using the priesthood, we must keep the commandments and live worthily. Power in the priesthood comes to us only from our Heavenly Father through the

Holy Ghost. With the power of the priesthood, we can do the Lord's work; without that power, we cannot.

- Show visual 1-a, "Priesthood holders administer to the sick today just as Christ did anciently."

"If we live for it, ours can be a power given us from our Heavenly Father that will bring peace to a troubled household. Ours can be a power that will bless and comfort little children, that will bring sleep to tearstained eyes in the wee hours of the morning. Ours can be the power that will bring happiness to a family home evening, the power to calm the unsettled nerves of a tired wife. Ours can be the power that will give direction to a confused and vulnerable teenager. Ours, the power to bless a daughter before she goes on her first date or before her temple marriage, or to bless a son before his departure for a mission or college. Ours, my young brethren, can be the power to stop evil thoughts of a group of boys gathered together in vulgar conversation. Ours can be the power to heal the sick and comfort the lonely. These are some of the important purposes of the priesthood" (H. Burke Peterson, in Conference Report, Apr. 1976, 50–51; or *Ensign,* May 1976, 33).

- Ask the assigned priesthood holder to share his experience showing the power of the priesthood in his life.

### Developing Power in the Priesthood

There are several things we can do to develop power in the priesthood:

#### Desire It

We must first have a desire to develop power in the priesthood. The scriptures teach that men receive from the Lord according to their desires (see Alma 29:4; D&C 4:3; 6:8; 7:1–3).

#### Live Righteously

We should strive to keep all the commandments of our Heavenly Father. By living righteously, we may have the Holy Ghost for our constant companion, and He will direct us to do the things we should do (see 2 Nephi 32:5). Righteous living includes learning to control our thoughts, words, and actions.

#### Be Humble

"He that truly humbleth himself, and repenteth of his sins, and endureth to the end, the same shall be blessed" (Alma 32:15). We should be willing to accept and follow our leaders' counsel, complete the assignments given to us by our priesthood leaders, and listen to and follow the promptings of the Spirit. Other ways we can show humility include (1) honestly considering the righteous desires of

*1-a, Priesthood holders administer to the sick today just as Christ did anciently.* (Christ Healing the Blind, *by Carl Bloch. Used by permission of the National Historic Museum at Frederiksborg in Hillerød.)*

family members, even though they may not be exactly the same as our desires; (2) listening—even to the smallest child; (3) putting the welfare of the family ahead of our own comfort; and (4) speaking in a voice that always reflects our love and concern for others.

## Study

We must search and ponder the scriptures. Only by studying the scriptures personally can we know God's will and live the gospel. We also need to study our priesthood manuals in order to know our specific duties as priesthood holders. President George Albert Smith taught, "It is your duty first of all to learn what the Lord wants and then by the power and strength of His holy Priesthood to [so] magnify your calling . . . that the people will be glad to follow you" (in Conference Report, Apr. 1942, 14).

## Pray

We must ask our Heavenly Father what He would have us do. We should always pray for guidance in using the priesthood correctly. Concerning the power of prayer, President Gordon B. Hinckley taught: "Prayer unlocks the powers of heaven in our behalf. Prayer is the great gift which our Eternal Father has given us by which we may approach Him and speak with Him in the name of the Lord Jesus Christ. Be prayerful. You cannot make it alone. You cannot reach your potential alone. You need the help of the Lord" (*Teachings of Gordon B. Hinckley* [1997], 470).

## Love Others

Jesus Christ has taught us that the power of the priesthood is founded on love and that we should love all people (see D&C 121:41–42, 45–46). Love begins at home. We should love our families and be concerned for their welfare. One way we show our love for our family members is by using the priesthood to direct and bless their lives.

### Use the Priesthood to Bless and Strengthen Our Families

When we use the priesthood, we are examples to other priesthood holders, to the world, and, perhaps most importantly, to our families. As our family members see us use the priesthood, they will know that we are servants of the Lord and will come to us when they need help. All families should experience the blessings which come when fathers and sons use the priesthood for the benefit of their families.

The priesthood can make a difference in our homes. President David O. McKay said, "A home is transformed because a man holds and honors the priesthood" ("Priesthood," *Instructor,* Oct. 1968, 378).

- In what ways have you or your family been blessed because of the priesthood?

## Conclusion

"We should all realize that there is nothing in the world more powerful than the priesthood of God" (N. Eldon Tanner, in Conference Report, Apr. 1976, 63; or *Ensign,* May 1976, 41).

In the following story, President N. Eldon Tanner explained the importance of being worthy to receive the priesthood:

"When I was a bishop I had six boys in my ward old enough to be ordained elders. I could only recommend five of them, because one of them wasn't ready. We had talked about it several times, and he had said to me, 'I am not worthy.' He felt very bad about it, but he didn't expect to be recommended. . . . His uncle came to me and said, 'You are surely not going to hold that boy back with his five friends going forward.' He pled with me to let him go. He said, 'You will be driving him out of the Church if you don't.'

"I explained to this man, 'The priesthood is the most important thing that we can give this boy. We are not handing the priesthood out. . . . This boy and I understand each other, and he is not ready to be ordained an elder.' And he wasn't recommended.

"A few years later I was attending a general conference . . . , and a young man came up to me and said, 'President Tanner, you wouldn't remember me. I am the boy whom you didn't recommend to be ordained an elder.' As he put his hand out, he said, 'I want to thank you for it. I am a bishop now in California. If you had recommended me when I wasn't worthy, I possibly never would have appreciated what the priesthood is and what is expected of one, and surely I would never have been a bishop as I am today' " (in Conference Report, Apr. 1973, 122; or *Ensign,* July 1973, 94).

We must all learn "that the rights of the priesthood are inseparably connected with the powers of heaven, and that the powers of heaven cannot be controlled nor handled only upon the principles of righteousness" (D&C 121:36). To receive power from God, we must become worthy of it.

We should always remember that we hold God's authority and power and that we represent Him. When we exercise the priesthood, we should ask ourselves, "What would Jesus Christ have me do in this situation? Am I acting the way He would have me act?"

## Challenges

Commit yourself to carefully study the instructions of this priesthood manual and to accept the challenges which are given in each lesson. By completing these challenges, you will develop power in the priesthood, become closer to our Heavenly Father, and be of greater service to others.

**Additional Scripture**

- Doctrine and Covenants 107:1–14 (differences between the Melchizedek Priesthood and the Aaronic Priesthood)

**Teacher Preparation**

Before presenting this lesson:

1. Study *Gospel Principles* chapters 13, "The Priesthood," and 14, "Priesthood Organization."

2. Study Doctrine and Covenants 121:34–46.

3. Assign a priesthood holder to share an experience he has had which demonstrates the power of the priesthood.

4. Ask each class member to bring his scriptures to priesthood meeting each week and to be prepared to read and mark the specific scriptures in each lesson.

5. Assign class members to present any stories, scriptures, or quotations you wish.

# THE PRIESTHOOD FROM ADAM TO THE RESTORATION

*L e s s o n  2*

The purpose of this lesson is to help us understand that the priesthood was given to Adam and other righteous men through the ages.

## Introduction

Adam was the first man on the earth to hold the priesthood. This means God gave him the authority to direct his family and perform the ordinances they needed to return to His presence. He was also the first prophet to receive the keys of presidency, or the authority to direct God's Church on earth. With this authority, he gave many men the priesthood and taught them how to use it. All the prophets of the Lord in each dispensation since Adam have held this same authority.

- Display visual 2-a, "The Priesthood in All Generations." Explain that the chart is divided into seven time periods called dispensations. Read the definition of a dispensation at the bottom of the chart. Explain that we do not know how many dispensations of the gospel there have been, but these seven represent some of the major ones. Refer to each appropriate picture as the dispensation is mentioned in the lesson and, as time permits, read the scriptures included with each picture.

### The Adamic Dispensation

- Refer to visual 2-a, "The Priesthood in All Generations." Point out the picture of the Adamic dispensation and read Doctrine and Covenants 107:40–41 as shown on the chart.

Soon after Adam and Eve were driven out of the Garden of Eden, an angel appeared to them and taught them the gospel (see Moses 5:6–9). The Church was also organized and Adam was baptized in water the same way we have been instructed to baptize today (see Moses 6:64–65). The priesthood was then given to Adam so that he could have authority to perform all of the ordinances of the gospel for his family. With this authority he baptized the members of his family and gave the priesthood to those of his sons who were righteous.

| MILLENNIUM |
| :---: |

| A.D. 1830 | **DISPENSATION OF THE FULNESS OF TIMES**<br>Joseph Smith and Other Latter-day Prophets<br>Church Restored (D&C 20:1) Priesthood Restored (D&C 13; 27:8, 12–13) |  |

**Great Apostasy**

| About A.D. 30 | **DISPENSATION OF THE MERIDIAN OF TIME**<br>Jesus Christ and His Apostles<br>(Matthew 16:19; Hebrews 5:5–10; 3 Nephi 11:19–22; 12:1) |  |

**Apostasy**

| About 1500 B.C. | **MOSAIC DISPENSATION**<br><br>(D&C 84:6) |  |

**Apostasy**

| About 2000 B.C. | **DISPENSATION OF ABRAHAM**<br><br>(D&C 84:14; Abraham 1:16, 18) |  |

**Apostasy**

| About 3000 B.C. | **DISPENSATION OF NOAH**<br><br>(Moses 8:19–20) |  |

**Apostasy**

| About 3765 B.C. | **DISPENSATION OF ENOCH**<br><br>(D&C 107:48, 53) |  |

**Apostasy**

| About 4000 B.C. | **ADAMIC DISPENSATION**<br><br>(D&C 107:40–41) |  |

Dispensation: A period of time in which the Lord has at least one authorized servant on earth who has the priesthood and the keys necessary to administer the gospel.

*2-a, The Priesthood in All Generations*
*"They who receive this priesthood receive me, saith the Lord" (D&C 84:35).*

All people have agency, or freedom to choose. With this agency, some of the children of Adam chose to break the commandments. As larger numbers of them made this choice and turned from the truth, they "began from that time forth to be carnal, sensual, and devilish" (see Moses 5:12–13). This kind of falling away from the truth is called an apostasy.

### The Dispensations of Enoch and Noah

Adam and those who kept the commandments preached to these people and tried to get them to repent. Most people did not repent, but those who did joined the prophet Enoch and were called Zion. The scriptures tell us that "Enoch and all his people walked with God, . . . and it came to pass that Zion was not, for God received it up into his own bosom" (Moses 7:69).

- Refer to the picture of the dispensation of Enoch on the chart and read Doctrine and Covenants 107:48, 53.

After Enoch and the people of Zion were taken from the earth, the wicked people became very numerous. The Lord sent the prophet Noah to warn them and call them to repentance. Noah told the wicked people that if they did not repent they would be swept off the earth in a great flood. Noah's family members, however, were the only ones who listened to him and kept the commandments. The flood came as Noah had warned, and he and his family were the only ones saved.

- Refer to the picture of the dispensation of Noah on the chart and read Moses 8:19–20.

### The Priesthood after the Flood

After the flood, Noah gave the priesthood to his righteous children and grandchildren. One righteous man who lived after Noah and who received the priesthood was Melchizedek. Melchizedek was so righteous that the priesthood was named after him (see D&C 107:2–4, which also explains that the priesthood was named after Melchizedek to avoid repeating the Lord's name too often). Melchizedek ordained Abraham to the priesthood, and Abraham ordained others. Thus, the Melchizedek Priesthood continued to the time of Moses.

- Refer to the picture of the dispensation of Abraham on the chart and read Doctrine and Covenants 84:14.

### Melchizedek Priesthood Taken from Israel

Abraham gave the priesthood to his son Isaac, and Isaac gave it to his son Jacob. Jacob's name was changed to Israel, and thereafter Jacob's descendants were known as the children of Israel.

In Moses' day, after he had led the children of Israel out of Egypt, the Lord offered the children of Israel the fulness of His gospel. They rejected it, however, so the Lord took away from them the Melchizedek Priesthood and the higher ordinances of the gospel. They were left with laws that were to direct the physical, or temporal, activities of the people. These laws were administered by the Aaronic Priesthood (named after Aaron, the brother of Moses). Most of these laws are found in the books of Exodus, Leviticus, and Deuteronomy in the Old Testament. They were not meant to replace the fulness of the gospel, but were given as a way to prepare the children of Israel to live the gospel in its fulness at a later time.

Even though the Melchizedek Priesthood was taken from Israel as a nation, it was not permanently taken from the earth. Between the time of Moses and the coming of Jesus Christ, several prophets held the Melchizedek Priesthood. Some of these prophets were Elijah, Isaiah, Jeremiah, Lehi, Daniel, and Ezekiel.

- Refer to the Mosaic dispensation pictured on the chart and read Doctrine and Covenants 84:6.

### The Priesthood in the Days of Jesus

When Jesus came to earth He restored the gospel in its fulness. He held the keys, or the full authority, of the priesthood and ordained Apostles (see Matthew 10:1–4) and Seventies (see Luke 10:1). He organized His Church among His followers, and when He finally left the earth, the Apostles were given the authority to ordain others to various offices in the priesthood (see Acts 14:23). In this way, the priesthood was passed on and remained the foundation of the Church of Jesus Christ.

- Refer to the chart and read Matthew 16:19; Hebrews 5:5–10; and 3 Nephi 11:19–22; 12:1.

### The Great Apostasy

For some time after Jesus ascended to heaven, the Church continued to teach the truth, and thousands of people from many cities joined the Church. However, in time some who had joined the Church refused to obey the laws and ordinances of the gospel and changed them to suit their own ways of thinking. Many members, including the Apostles and other priesthood leaders, were persecuted and killed. As these men were killed and others fell away from the truth, the Church lost the authority of the priesthood. Eventually, the priesthood no longer remained in the Church.

For many centuries, the fulness of the gospel was not on the earth. Those churches which were organized during the Apostasy did not have the priesthood. As a result, they could not receive direction from God or perform the ordinances of salvation. As Isaiah said they would, they "transgressed the laws, changed the ordinance, [and broke] the everlasting covenant" (see Isaiah 24:5).

## The Restoration of the Priesthood

One day, in the spring of 1820, a young man named Joseph Smith prayed to God about which church he should join. In answer to his prayer, God the Father and His Son, Jesus Christ, appeared to him. Jesus told him to join none of the churches, saying, "They draw near to me with their lips, but their hearts are far from me, they teach for doctrines the commandments of men, having a form of godliness, but they deny the power thereof" (Joseph Smith—History 1:19).

Through Joseph Smith, the Lord brought back to the earth His true Church and restored all the necessary principles and ordinances of His gospel. The Lord gave to Joseph Smith the holy priesthood, which was held by Adam and other righteous men through the ages. We have that priesthood today, and the Lord has promised that in this dispensation, the dispensation of the fulness of times, the priesthood will not be taken away again. It will be here when Christ returns to earth.

- Refer to the picture of the dispensation of the fulness of times on the chart, and read Doctrine and Covenants 13; 20:1; 27:8, 12–13.

**Conclusion**

- Show visual 2-b, "Men are given the priesthood by the laying on of hands by those who have been given authority of God."

The priesthood which worthy male members of the Church hold today is the same priesthood given to Adam and the other prophets through the ages. It is the power and authority of God, and we are His representatives on the earth. Because we are His representatives, we hold the power to help ourselves, our families, and others return to God's presence. When given permission by the bishop or branch president, we can baptize, give the gift of the Holy Ghost, and ordain others to the priesthood. In these and other ways the priesthood can bring joy into our lives and the lives of others.

**Challenges**

Discuss the priesthood with your family. Develop ways you can help your sons be worthy to receive the priesthood. Strive to be an example of a worthy priesthood bearer.

At the proper time, and when you are authorized to do so, baptize and confirm your children and ordain your sons to the priesthood.

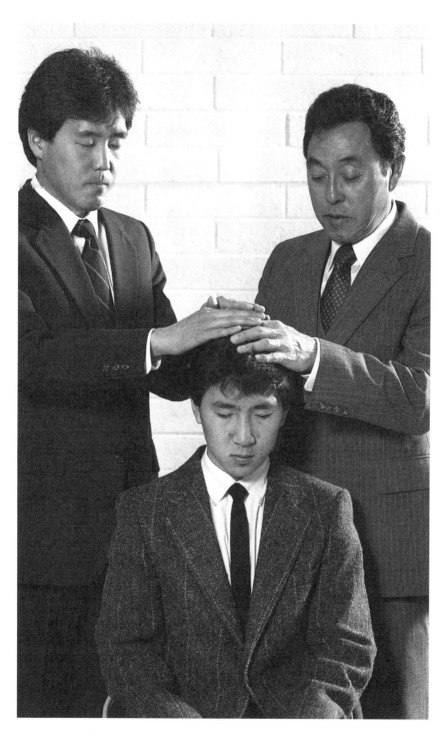

*2-b, Men are given the priesthood by the laying on of hands*
*by those who have been given authority of God.*

**Teacher Preparation**

Before presenting this lesson:

1. Study *Gospel Principles* chapter 14, "Priesthood Organization."

2. Assign class members to present any stories, scriptures, or quotations you wish.

# THE RESTORATION OF THE PRIESTHOOD

*Lesson 3*

The purpose of this lesson is to help us understand the restoration of the holy priesthood, which was taken from the earth after the time of Christ.

## Introduction

As priesthood bearers, we hold the same authority that God gave to His servants in the past.

- Display visual 3-a, "Christ ordained twelve Apostles and gave them the keys of the priesthood."

The following are some of the ordinances we can perform with the priesthood:

1. Baptize, as John the Baptist and the Nephites did (see Matthew 3:15–17 and 3 Nephi 11:19–26).

2. Administer the sacrament, as Jesus did (see Luke 22:19–20).

3. Bestow the Holy Ghost, as Paul and the Nephites did (see Acts 19:5–6 and 3 Nephi 18:37).

4. Heal the sick, as Peter did (see Acts 3:1–8).

These priesthood ordinances were performed in the past by many faithful priesthood holders. We can perform priesthood duties today because God's priesthood is again on earth. Worthy men in His Church have been given the same priesthood that His ancient servants held.

## The Great Apostasy and the Restoration

As discussed in lesson 2, the Apostasy took place after the time of Christ. Because of the wickedness of men, the priesthood and most of the true teachings of Jesus Christ were changed or lost. Many great prophets had foretold that the time would come when the people would fall away from the truth. One such prophet was Isaiah. Speaking of the Apostasy, he said that the people "have transgressed the laws, changed the ordinance, broken the everlasting covenant"

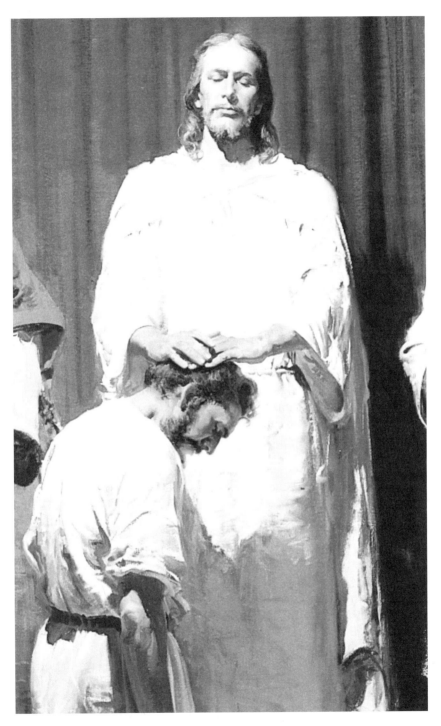

*3-a, Christ ordained twelve Apostles and gave them the keys of the priesthood.*

(Isaiah 24:5). Isaiah's prophecy was fulfilled. Because of transgression, after the time of Christ the true order of the priesthood was taken from the earth. The Book of Mormon people were for a time the only people to enjoy the blessings of the priesthood, but finally even they fell away from the truth. Because of the Apostasy, the people on the earth could no longer hear the true gospel and receive the saving ordinances of the priesthood.

Heavenly Father wants all His children to return to Him. It was necessary, therefore, for Him to restore the priesthood and its ordinances and all other truths necessary for us to return to Him.

Many prophets looked forward to the Restoration. Isaiah, for example, prophesied of a time when the Lord would "do a marvellous work among this people, even a marvellous work and a wonder" (Isaiah 29:13–14). Peter also foretold of the time when there would be a "restitution of all things" (see Acts 3:19–21). Restitution means to bring back something that has been taken or lost. The priesthood and the gospel had to be restored or all mankind would have been lost. This restoration began in 1820 when God the Father and the Lord Jesus Christ appeared to Joseph Smith.

### Joseph Smith and the Restoration of the Priesthood

Joseph Smith was one of the "noble and great" spirit children of our Heavenly Father. Like Abraham, he was chosen before he came to earth for a very important mission. (See Abraham 3:22–23.) As a result, Joseph Smith's mission was foretold by many of the early prophets. Both Joseph of Egypt and Lehi, the Book of Mormon prophet, knew about Joseph Smith and his mission. Lehi spoke to his son Joseph of a prophecy made by Joseph of Egypt about a latter-day prophet who was also named Joseph.

- Read 2 Nephi 3:6–15.

Joseph Smith began his search for truth at a very young age. When he was only 14, he went to a grove of trees and asked God to tell him which church to join. As a result of his prayer, God and Jesus Christ appeared to him and instructed him. Three years later, in 1823, the angel Moroni appeared to Joseph Smith and told him about the Book of Mormon. Eventually, Moroni gave Joseph Smith this sacred record of the former inhabitants of America. With the help of God, Joseph was able to translate the record. The Book of Mormon and the revelations given to Joseph Smith restored many of the truths which had been lost during the Apostasy.

But the restoration of the truth about God and His doctrines was not enough. Joseph Smith was born when the priesthood was not on the earth. Because he could not fulfill his mission without the priesthood, it was necessary that the priesthood be restored to him by those who held the keys, or the authority to ordain him. In 1838 Joseph Smith recorded the following about how he and Oliver Cowdery received the Aaronic Priesthood.

■ Display visual 3-b, "The Aaronic Priesthood and the Melchizedek Priesthood were restored on the banks of the Susquehanna River."

"We . . . continued the work of translation, when, in the ensuing month (May, 1829), we on a certain day went into the woods to pray and inquire of the Lord respecting baptism for the remission of sins, that we found mentioned in the translation of the plates. While we were . . . praying and calling upon the Lord, a messenger from heaven descended in a cloud of light, and having laid his hands upon us, he ordained us [to the Priesthood of Aaron]. . . .

"The messenger who visited us on this occasion and conferred this Priesthood upon us, said that his name was John, the same that is called John the Baptist in the New Testament, and that he acted under the direction of Peter, James and John, who held the keys of the Priesthood of Melchizedek, which Priesthood, he said, would in due time be conferred on us. . . . It was on the fifteenth day of May, 1829, that we were ordained under the hand of this messenger, and baptized" (see Joseph Smith—History 1:68–72; see also D&C 13).

Later in that same year, 1829, Joseph Smith and Oliver Cowdery were given the Melchizedek Priesthood. Jesus' ancient Apostles Peter, James, and John appeared to them, laid their hands upon their heads, and ordained them (see D&C 27:12). Thus, Joseph Smith received both the Aaronic Priesthood and the Melchizedek Priesthood. The priesthood authority had been restored: those who had held it in earlier times had brought back to the earth the power of God.

### The Aaronic Priesthood

"The Aaronic Priesthood is an 'appendage to the greater, or Melchizedek Priesthood' (D&C 107:14). It is named after Aaron, Moses' brother, because it was conferred on him and his seed. Brethren who hold the Aaronic Priesthood have authority to administer in ordinances such as baptism and blessing and passing the sacrament. (See D&C 107:13–14, 20.)

"The mission of the Aaronic Priesthood is to help those who hold it to—

"Become converted to the gospel of Jesus Christ and live by its teachings.

*3-b, The Aaronic Priesthood and the Melchizedek Priesthood were restored on the banks of the Susquehanna River.*

"Magnify their priesthood callings.

"Give meaningful service.

"Prepare to receive the Melchizedek Priesthood.

"Prepare to serve full-time missions.

"Live worthy to receive temple covenants and be worthy husbands and fathers.

"When the Aaronic Priesthood is conferred on a man, he is ordained to an office in that priesthood. These offices are deacon, teacher, and priest. Brethren who hold the same office are organized into a quorum. Each quorum is presided over by a president who teaches the members their duties and encourages brotherhood among them" (*Priesthood Leader's Guidebook* [1992], 6–7).

The Aaronic Priesthood is a preparatory priesthood. It prepares the way for those who administer the blessings of the Melchizedek Priesthood, and it gives Aaronic Priesthood holders the experience they need to receive the Melchizedek Priesthood.

- What can Aaronic Priesthood holders do to prepare themselves to receive the Melchizedek Priesthood? How can Melchizedek Priesthood holders help them?

**The Melchizedek Priesthood**

The Melchizedek Priesthood is named for Melchizedek, who lived in the days of the Old Testament prophet Abraham. Before his day it was called the Holy Priesthood after the Order of the Son of God. But to avoid repeating the name of God too often, the Church was instructed to call the priesthood after Melchizedek "because Melchizedek was such a great high priest" (see D&C 107:1–6).

The Doctrine and Covenants reveals that the Melchizedek Priesthood has the right of presidency over all offices in the Church. Brethren holding the Melchizedek Priesthood have the authority needed to lead in the Church and oversee the preaching of the gospel. They also have the authority to preside over wards, branches, stakes, and missions. There exists no higher authority or priesthood. In addition, this priesthood has the authority to administer all the spiritual ordinances necessary for us to return to our Heavenly Father. (See D&C 107:8–19.)

Some of the powers and duties of the Melchizedek Priesthood include:

Bestowing the gift of the Holy Ghost.

Ordaining worthy men to the Melchizedek Priesthood.

Performing temple work for the living and the dead.

Administering to the sick.

Attending to the spiritual and temporal welfare of all people.

The Melchizedek Priesthood offices of elder, high priest, patriarch, Seventy, and Apostle vary only with regard to their specific responsibilities. Melchizedek Priesthood holders may perform all the duties of the Aaronic Priesthood. Through the Melchizedek Priesthood, we prepare ourselves and others to someday enter the kingdom of heaven.

- Invite class members to discuss some of the blessings they enjoy because the priesthood has been restored. Invite them also to think about how they might more fully enjoy all of the blessings that are available through the priesthood.

**Conclusion**

Elder Ezra Taft Benson said: "God has again spoken from the heavens. The priesthood and authority to act in His name have been restored again to men on the earth, following centuries of darkness. The fulness of the everlasting gospel is here with all of its saving principles" (*The Teachings of Ezra Taft Benson* [1988], 113).

If the priesthood were not on the earth, we could not do God's work, and the true Church could not exist. Consequently, no one could gain eternal life. Eternal life comes only to those who keep the principles and ordinances of the gospel, and the ordinances of the gospel cannot be performed without the priesthood. Because the priesthood is God's power and not man's, man cannot give himself the priesthood. Nor can he confer it on others unless he has received it by proper authority (see D&C 42:11). For these reasons the priesthood was restored to Joseph Smith by heavenly messengers. Today the priesthood is found in the true Church of Jesus Christ, which was restored to perform the Lord's work for the benefit of all mankind (see D&C 84:17).

Any male member of the Church who has received the priesthood of God has a great responsibility to help himself, his family, and all people around him receive the blessings of eternal life.

**Challenges**

Learn the opportunities and duties of the priesthood. You may do this by reading the scriptures, fasting and praying, studying your priesthood manual, and receiving instruction from your priesthood leaders.

Perform your duties in the priesthood to the best of your ability and always seek to improve.

Support those in authority over you, being careful not to assume any power or authority not given to you.

**Teacher Preparation**

Before presenting this lesson:

1. Read Doctrine and Covenants 13, 20, 84, 107, 121, and 124 to gain a better understanding of the priesthood.

2. Study *Gospel Principles* chapters 14, "Priesthood Organization," and 17, "The Church of Jesus Christ Today."

3. Assign class members to present any stories, scriptures, or quotations you wish.

# THE PRIESTHOOD QUORUM

*L e s s o n   4*

The purpose of this lesson is to help us understand the ways that priesthood quorums can help individuals, families, and the Church.

**Introduction**

Begin the lesson with "Let Us All Press On" (*Hymns,* no. 243; or *Gospel Principles,* 318).

As priesthood holders, we have the freedom and responsibility to do many things on our own without being told to do them by Church leaders (see D&C 58:26–29). We can do our work; we can care for family members; we can be obedient and do many good things for ourselves, our families, and others. However, we should all recognize that at times we will need help from someone else. We might be stuck in the mud, sick with no strength to go for help, brokenhearted at the disobedience of a child, or discouraged because no one seems to care. The following story illustrates the importance of asking others for help when we need it:

One day a farmer was preparing to gather his hay into his barn when he saw a heavy rainstorm approaching. If he could not gather it before the rain, the hay would be ruined. He needed immediate help. He asked his neighbors for assistance, and they helped him gather the hay before the rain could harm it. Because of their help, he was able to save his crop.

When we have individual or family problems that we cannot solve alone, we should not be afraid to ask others for help.

- Who could we ask for help in times of need?

**The Definition and Purpose of Priesthood Quorums**

A priesthood quorum is an organized group of brethren who hold the same office in the priesthood. In some units of the Church where few men hold the priesthood, all the priesthood holders may meet together for priesthood instruction.

In units of the Church where many men hold the priesthood, quorums of high priests, elders, priests, teachers, and deacons are organized. Each quorum, except the priests quorum, is presided over by a president and two counselors. The priests quorum is presided over by the bishop with two priests as his assistants. The stake president and his counselors are the presidency of the high priests quorum for all of the high priests in the stake.

Heavenly Father established priesthood quorums to help priesthood bearers come together to learn how to magnify the priesthood and to receive other gospel instruction. Each Sunday, to help quorum members meet their obligation to help each other and teach each other their responsibilities, quorum meetings are held. The purposes of these meetings are to teach the gospel, teach priesthood responsibilities, conduct quorum business, discuss the needs of the quorum or ward, share testimonies, and build unity.

The scriptures tell us how to fulfill our priesthood responsibilities and duties.

▪ Read Doctrine and Covenants 107:99–100.

The quorum presidencies or group leaders are responsible for teaching us our priesthood duties and for giving us opportunities to learn as we perform these duties. After we learn our duties, our responsibility is to act diligently in our appointed office in the priesthood. As we magnify our priesthood callings by serving others and accepting assignments from our quorum presidencies, we increase our understanding and our ability to serve.

▪ Have the members discuss some priesthood duties they have learned and then performed.

**How Priesthood Quorums Function**

Priesthood quorums function according to principles that help quorum members more fully live the gospel and enjoy the blessings of membership in a quorum. Some of these principles are righteousness, unity, assistance, and friendship.

*Righteousness*

The Lord has said that "the rights of the priesthood are inseparably connected with the powers of heaven, and that the powers of heaven cannot be controlled nor handled only upon the principles of righteousness" (D&C 121:36). The strength of our priesthood quorum depends on the strength of its members. The more righteous we become, the more power and guidance we will receive from the Lord.

### Unity

In order to accomplish their purposes, priesthood quorums must be unified. "The quorum should be so united that we can help one another, not only spiritually but also financially and in every other way. If we can get the spirit of unity in our quorums, then we are beginning to understand the full meaning of our priesthood organization in the Church" (David O. McKay, "The Fundamental Basis for Home Teaching," *Improvement Era,* July 1963, 615).

### Assistance

One of the most important purposes of priesthood quorums is to encourage quorum members to serve one another. "All priesthood quorums are . . . 'commanded' [by the Lord] to marshal their forces and, under the spirit and power of the Priesthood, to see to it that every person who is in distress is assisted by his quorum to become self-sustaining" (Harold B. Lee, "The Place of the Priesthood Quorum in the Church Security Program," *Improvement Era,* Oct. 1937, 634).

President J. Reuben Clark Jr. listed several examples of how we can assist each other. He said: "[Quorum] assistance may take the form of helping the needy brother in his actual need and problem, to build a home, or to start in a small business, or, if he be an artisan, to get him a kit of tools, or, if he be a farmer, to get him seeds, or to help him plant or harvest a crop, or to meet some urgent credit need he has, or to supply him with clothing, or shelter, or food, or medical assistance, or schooling for the children, or to give aid in any number of other ways" ("Church Welfare Plan" [A discussion before the First Citizens' Conference on Government Management at Estes Park, Colorado, 20 June 1939], 20).

### Friendship

In the early days of the Church, men gave to their quorums "their undivided, loyal allegiance. . . . We shall never know the full strength and beauty of the friendships created in those priesthood [quorums]. Men cared for each other's families when missions were undertaken. Privations and sorrows were shared, and loyalties were created. . . . Men offered their very lives for each other. . . .

"It is true, we are not exposed to the same physical dangers which once existed, but we are beset by innumerable other hazards which I fear are sometimes worse in their ultimate consequences than those that confronted our forebears. Do we need friends to meet these situations? We do!" (Stephen L. Richards, "The Priesthood Quorum: A Three-Fold Definition," *Improvement Era,* May 1939, 294).

It should be a source of comfort to us to know that if we ever need strengthening in the gospel, all the faithful brethren in our quorum would unite to warn us, to strengthen us spiritually, and to help us find our way back into activity. Elder Boyd K. Packer said: "A man who becomes inactive does not lose his membership in the quorum. He may lose interest in the quorum, but the quorum must never lose interest in him. The quorum is responsible always and continually for each of its members. To ignore an inactive member, to withdraw interest in and contact with him is [to do away with] his rights as a holder of the priesthood" (*A Royal Priesthood* [Melchizedek Priesthood personal study guide, 1975], 134).

The Church needs "every member, that all may be edified together, that the system may be kept perfect" (D&C 84:110). Priesthood quorums are a vital part of the Church organization. As the priesthood quorum carries out its responsibilities, every member of the quorum must be considered. Elder Packer said: "If his priesthood quorum functions properly, a man [or boy] sustained by the brethren of his quorum, almost could not fail in any phase of life's responsibility" (*A Royal Priesthood* [1975], 134).

The quorum operates properly when each quorum member does his part. By serving as home teachers, for example, priesthood holders serve as links between the quorum president and each family in the quorum. As problems are identified and needs are reported by the home teachers, the quorum can move into action. With this information, the quorum, under the direction of the priesthood quorum presidency, can help quorum members in need. After the family, the quorum is the first source of help for those in need.

- What are some specific ways priesthood quorum members can serve each other?

- Have the members read and mark Doctrine and Covenants 108:7. What does this scripture tell us we can do to strengthen each other? (List the answers on the chalkboard.)

### Doing Our Part as Members of a Priesthood Quorum

One purpose of the priesthood quorum is to help each priesthood bearer learn how to use the priesthood and help his fellow quorum members in time of need. This purpose is best carried out if each member is willing to help and if the specific needs of quorum members are identified. For this reason, we must keep our quorum leaders informed about the needs we see and be willing to ask for help ourselves when we are in need. Quorum members cannot help others until they know of their needs. Each priesthood holder should try to solve his own problems, but times come when we need the help of the quorum. We should not feel ashamed to ask for help, because this will provide an opportunity for others to be of service.

The following story demonstrates how a quorum helped one of its members:

"In the autumn of 1918, that terribly climactic year of World War I during which more than 14 million people died of that awful scourge 'the black plague,' or Spanish influenza, . . . winter came early . . . and froze much of the sugar beet crop in the ground. My dad and brother Francis were desperately trying to get out of the frosty ground one load of beets each day which they would plow out of the ground, cut off the tops, and toss the beets, one at a time, into the huge red beet wagon and then haul the load off to the sugar factory. It was slow and tedious work due to the frost and the lack of farm help, since my brother Floyd and I were in the army. . . .

"While they were thusly engaged in harvesting the family's only cash crop and were having their evening meal one day, a phone call came through from our eldest brother, George Albert, . . . bearing the tragic news that Kenneth, nine-year-old son of our brother Charles, . . . had been stricken with the dread 'flu,' and after only a few hours of violent sickness, had died on his father's lap; and would dad please come to Ogden and bring the boy home and lay him away in the family plot in the Lehi Cemetery.

"My father . . . headed for Five Points in Ogden to bring his little grandson home for burial. When he arrived at the home he found 'Charl' sprawled across the cold form of his dear one, . . . virtually burning up with fever.

" 'Take my boy home,' muttered the stricken young father, 'and lay him away in the family lot and come back for me tomorrow.'

"Father brought Kenneth home, made a coffin in his carpenter shop, and mother and our sisters . . . placed a cushion and a lining in it, and then dad went with Franz and two kind neighbors to dig the grave. So many were dying the families had to do the grave digging. A brief graveside service was all that was permitted.

"The folks had scarcely returned from the cemetery when the telephone rang again and George Albert (Bert) was on the line with another terrifying message: Charl had died and two of his beautiful little girls—Vesta, 7, and Elaine, 5—were critically ill, and two babies—Raeldon, 4, and Pauline, 3—had been stricken.

"Our good cousins . . . were able to get a casket for Charl and they sent him home in a railroad baggage car. Father and young Franz brought the body from the railroad station. . . .

"Next day my sturdy, unconquerable old dad was called on still another of his grim missions—this time to bring home Vesta, the smiling one with the raven hair and big blue eyes.

"When he arrived at the home he found Juliett, the grief-crazed mother, kneeling at the crib of darling little Elaine, the blue-eyed baby angel with the golden curls. Juliett was sobbing wearily and praying. . . .

"Before father arrived home with Vesta the dread word had come again. Elaine had gone to join her daddy, brother Kenneth, and sister Vesta. And so it was that father made another heartbreaking journey to bring home and lay away a fourth member of his family, all within the week.

"The telephone did not ring the evening of the day they laid away Elaine nor were there any more sad tidings of death the next morning. . . .

"After breakfast dad said to Franz, 'Well, son, we had better get down to the field and see if we can get another load of beets out of the ground before they get frozen in any tighter. Hitch up and let's be on our way.'

"Francis drove the four-horse outfit down the driveway and dad climbed aboard. As they drove along the Saratoga Road, they passed wagon after wagon-load of beets being hauled to the factory and driven by neighborhood farmers. As they passed by, each driver would wave a greeting: 'Hi ya, Uncle George,' 'Sure sorry, George,' 'Tough break, George,' 'You've got a lot of friends, George.'

"On the last wagon was . . . Jasper Rolfe. He waved a cheery greeting and called out: 'That's all of 'em, Uncle George.'

"My dad turned to Francis and said: 'I wish it was all of ours.'

"When they arrived at the farm gate, Francis jumped down off the big red beet wagon and opened the gate as we drove onto the field. He pulled up, stopped the team, paused a moment and scanned the field, from left to right and back and forth—and lo and behold, there wasn't a sugar beet on the whole field. Then it dawned upon him what Jasper Rolfe meant when he called out: 'That's all of 'em, Uncle George!'

"Then dad got down off the wagon, picked up a handful of the rich, brown soil he loved so much, and then in his thumbless left hand a beet top, and he looked for a moment at these symbols of his labor, as if he couldn't believe his eyes.

"Then father sat down on a pile of beet tops—this man who brought four of his loved ones home for burial in the course of only six days; made caskets, dug graves, and even helped with the burial clothing— this amazing man who never faltered, nor flinched, nor wavered throughout this agonizing ordeal—sat down on a pile of beet tops and sobbed like a little child.

"Then he arose, wiped his eyes with his big, red bandanna handker-chief, looked up at the sky, and said: 'Thanks, Father, for the elders of our ward' " (Les Goates, quoted by Vaughn J. Featherstone, in Conference Report, Apr. 1973, 46–48; or *Ensign,* July 1973, 36–37).

## Conclusion

All of the quorums of the Church are organized to accomplish the purposes of the Lord. As bearers of the priesthood, we must fulfill the responsibilities we are given.

President Joseph Fielding Smith wrote: "Never before in the history of the Church has the responsibility which has been given to the priesthood been more necessary of fulfilment than today. Never before have we been under greater obligation to serve the Lord, and keep his commandments, and magnify the callings which have been assigned to us" (*Doctrines of Salvation,* comp. Bruce R. McConkie, 3 vols. [1954–56], 3:117).

## Challenges

Fulfill the priesthood assignments given to you.

Be aware of the needs of other quorum members.

Seek help from your priesthood quorum when you need help.

### Teacher Preparation

Before presenting this lesson:

1. Read Doctrine and Covenants 107:21–26, 58–66, 85–100.

2. Assign class members to present any stories, scriptures, or quotations you wish.

# DUTIES OF THE DEACON

*L e s s o n    5*

---

The purpose of this lesson is to help us understand the duties of deacons.

**Introduction**

A Presiding Bishop of the Church gave the following counsel to the deacons of the Church:

"All men are children of God, but you have something more. You have the authority to act in his name. This sets you apart from the rest of the world. It does not automatically make you better than others, but it gives you the responsibility to live a better life than others.

"Because you know you are a child of God and hold his priesthood, more is expected of you than of those who do not have this great blessing" (Victor L. Brown, in Conference Report, Apr. 1972, 101; or *Ensign*, July 1972, 90).

**The Duties of a Deacon**

As deacons we are on the Lord's errand (see D&C 64:29). The Lord's work is our work. When we perform our priesthood duties, we honor the Savior. One of the best ways we can show our love for the Savior is by performing our duties as deacons. Some of these duties include the following.

▪ Display a poster of the following list, or write the information on the chalkboard:

---

Duties of a Deacon

1. Pass the sacrament.
2. Watch over the Church.
3. Warn, expound, exhort, and teach, and invite all to come unto Christ.
4. Assist the bishop with temporal things.
5. Fellowship quorum members and other young men.

---

*5-a, Passing the sacrament is a sacred responsibility.*

*Pass the Sacrament*

One of the most sacred duties we have as deacons is to pass the sacrament. When we do this, we should feel the Spirit of the Lord and the importance of the ordinance. We should be worthy to give the sacrament to the Saints as representatives of the Lord. We should act and dress as He would want us to.

One General Authority recalled his service as a deacon in these words: "I remember how I considered it an honor to participate in such a sacred service [the sacrament]. I remember so well how my parents taught me that my hands and heart should be clean and pure so that I would be worthy to participate in this ordinance" (Victor L. Brown, in Conference Report, Apr. 1972, 101; or *Ensign,* July 1972, 89–90).

When we pass the sacrament in the proper manner, we fulfill another duty of a deacon. That duty is to edify or to build up one another (see D&C 107:85). By seeing our devotion to this duty, the members will be edified and will have a greater desire to perform their duties.

▪ Show visual 5-a, "Passing the sacrament is a sacred responsibility."

*Watch Over the Church and Warn, Expound, Exhort, and Teach*

One of the ways we can watch over the Church is to help the members keep the commandments.

▪ How can we help members keep the commandments? (We can teach them the gospel by our words and actions.)

▪ Have class members read Doctrine and Covenants 20:58–59. What are some ways we can warn, teach, and invite all to come to Christ?

As we warn, invite, and teach others, we can help meet the spiritual needs of the members of the Church. One way we do this is by speaking in Church meetings. When we prayerfully prepare our talks, the Holy Ghost will witness the truth of our words to the members. Other ways we can fulfill these duties are notifying members of meetings, sharing the gospel, and bearing testimony.

*Assist the Bishop with Temporal Things*

Deacons help the bishop look after the temporal needs of the Church. This could include gathering fast offerings, helping to care for those in need, and helping to care for the meetinghouse and grounds.

The following story about gathering fast offerings shows how one young deacon learned the importance of this responsibility. This experience took place many years ago when members contributed food, clothing, and fuel as fast offerings to be distributed to those in need.

"As a deacon, I was assigned to gather the 'fast' on our block. A bewhiskered, beyond-middle-aged gentleman, Brother Peter Reid, was the supervisor, and it was his responsibility to see that the fast offerings were gathered and distributed to the needy. . . .

"I was to visit every home on the block . . . and give them the opportunity to give something for the benefit of the poor. One home would give a large lump of coal, another some wood, another a scoop of flour, a bottle of fruit, a cup of sugar, a slab of bacon, and so forth. . . .

"On a particular Saturday our football team had scheduled a game and I was eager to play. I knew it was my duty to gather the 'fast' and it would be wrong if I failed, but I wanted more than anything else to play that game. I chose pleasure over duty, and played football. . . .

"Early the next morning Brother Reid knocked on our back door and asked for me. I was conscience stricken—I wanted to run and hide—but I faced him, head down. All he said was: 'Willard, do you have time to take a little walk with me?'

"It was a cold fall day.

"I went with him, first to a little frame court near the corner of First North and Third West streets. He gently rapped on one of the doors and a poor little thin lady answered the door.

"She said: 'Brother Reid, we didn't get our food yesterday and we haven't a thing in the house to eat.'

"Brother Reid said: 'I'm sorry, sister, but I'm sure we'll have something for you before the close of the day.'

"We went to another door near the upper end of the court. In response to our knock a voice called for us to come in.

"We entered to find an aged man and his wife in bed. He said: 'Brother Reid, we are without coal, and we have to stay in bed to keep warm.'

"In another part of the court we were greeted by a little mother with her small children huddled together. The baby was crying and the other children had tear-stained faces.

"That was enough! . . .

"I was about to cry—overwhelmed by my appalling neglect of duty. . . . Those people had their food and coal early that afternoon—and I learned a most valuable lesson" (Willard R. Smith, quoted in "Program Outline for Teaching Observance of the Law of the Fast" [1965], 19–20).

Gathering fast offerings is only one way to help with the temporal needs of the Church and its members. Another way might be to help a

5-b, One of the duties of deacons is to collect fast offerings.

widow plant her garden, water it, and weed it. During harvest time we could help her gather and store the food. By doing these things we are helping her meet her temporal needs.

- Show visuals 5-b, "One of the duties of deacons is to collect fast offerings," and 5-c, "Working as a quorum on a welfare project is one way deacons watch over the Church."

### Fellowship Quorum Members and Other Young Men

We can fulfill this duty by encouraging each other to participate in quorum meetings and activities. We should also be concerned for the spiritual and temporal welfare of quorum members and do all we can to support them.

- Invite class members to think about the following question without answering aloud: Who are some of the young men I could help to fellowship and strengthen?

### How Deacons Learn Their Duties

As deacons we can learn our duties in many ways and places. One way we can learn them is through personal scripture study and prayer. To do this, we may have to find a time and a place where we can be alone to study our duties as explained in the scriptures and pray for help in understanding them.

We also learn our duties at home from our parents or older brothers. These duties can be taught during family home evening. This instruction is also taught on Sundays in priesthood meetings by the deacons quorum president. The Lord has commanded the deacons quorum president to preside over the deacons in his quorum and to teach them their duties (see D&C 107:85). The deacons quorum president can help us understand our duties and how to act in the office of a deacon. He is taught these duties by a priesthood adviser or a member of the bishopric or branch presidency.

One of the best ways to learn our duties is to perform them. When we perform our duties, we understand them better and please the Lord. And when the Lord is pleased with us, He will reveal many things to us through the Holy Ghost. As deacons we should always live worthy to have the Holy Ghost with us.

### How the Deacons Quorum Helps Deacons

Quorum members can help each other in many ways. As we meet together during quorum meeting, we can fellowship each other. We can also help each other learn our duties and plan activities that will help us perform them. Our duties include helping members meet their temporal needs, preparing for and giving missionary service, doing

*5-c, Working as a quorum on a welfare project is one way
deacons watch over the Church.*

family history work and being baptized for the dead, activating young men of quorum age, and learning the gospel. The quorum gives us the opportunity to work together in fulfilling these duties. And by doing our duty, we help build the kingdom of God.

Through our quorum service we can also experience personal growth in the gospel. We grow in knowledge as we study the gospel and fulfill our responsibilities, and we increase our leadership abilities by serving as officers in the quorum.

- Ask class members to read Doctrine and Covenants 107:60–62, 85. Who is to preside over a deacons quorum? What are his duties?

Those in authority over us select the president of the quorum and call him to serve. The president then selects two counselors, who must be approved and called by those in authority. The quorum adviser trains the officers in their duties. He also teaches the gospel lesson in the quorum meeting. The quorum officers instruct the members of the quorum in their priesthood duties. In these and similar ways, quorum members learn how to watch over the Church.

The deacons quorum also provides a place where we can receive friendship and help. If we are discouraged or unsure of the truth, we can receive encouragement and find answers to our problems from the quorum. The following story illustrates how we can build each other up by showing our concern for each other. In this case, the concern was shown for a less-active member of the quorum.

One deacon was less active in the Church. On Sundays he would usually work around the house. On many of these occasions, he wondered about priesthood meeting and felt a need for fellowship. But because no one ever extended an invitation to him to attend priesthood, he never felt wanted. One Sunday while he was painting a room in his home, the presidency of the deacons quorum visited him. They asked him if he would like to attend priesthood the next Sunday. He said no. His answer could have discouraged them, but they refused to give up. The three of them continued to visit him every Sunday with the same offer.

Although this less-active boy never did attend church as a deacon, the love and concern of the quorum presidency built him up and made a deep impression on him. This concern motivated him when he was older to seek out the Church. Today he is active in the Church and performing his priesthood duties.

### Conclusion

When we learn our duties and magnify the priesthood as deacons, we are strengthened and we help others live the gospel. This is what it means "to watch over the church, to be standing ministers unto the church" (D&C 84:111).

## Challenges

Live the gospel and be a good example of a priesthood holder.

Be reverent during the sacrament service; and when passing the sacrament, act and dress as a representative of the Savior should act and dress.

Collect fast offerings when asked to do so.

Study and pray about the scriptures that teach us the duties of the deacon.

## Additional Scriptures

- 1 Timothy 3:8–10 (the qualifications of deacons)

- Doctrine and Covenants 84:30–32 (office of deacon as an appendage to the lesser priesthood)

## Teacher Preparation

Before presenting this lesson:

1. Read Doctrine and Covenants 20:38–60; 107:1–100.

2. Prepare the poster suggested in the lesson, or write the information on the chalkboard.

3. Assign class members to present any stories, scriptures, or quotations you wish.

# DUTIES OF THE TEACHER

*Lesson 6*

The purpose of this lesson is to help us understand the duties of teachers.

## The Duties of a Teacher

Worthy brethren may be ordained teachers when they are at least 14 years old. A teacher has all the responsibilities of a deacon. He also has additional responsibilities. Since some of us are teachers and others will be someday, we should learn the duties of that office.

- Ask class members to read Doctrine and Covenants 20:53. What are some of the duties of a teacher? (List the responses on the chalkboard.)

To be with the members and strengthen them means to get to know them, to participate with them in Church activities, to teach them, to help them fulfill their needs, and to help them serve others.

- Ask class members to read Doctrine and Covenants 20:54–55. What are some other duties of the teacher? (List these on the chalkboard.)

Verse 54 tells us that teachers are to "see that there is no iniquity in the church, neither hardness with each other, neither lying, backbiting, nor evil speaking." Verse 55 tells us that teachers are also supposed to help members do their duty.

## How Does a Teacher Fulfill His Duties?

There are many ways a teacher can fulfill his responsibilities. For example, he can set a proper example, be a good home teacher, greet the members at church, prepare the sacrament, help at home, and be a peacemaker.

### Set a Proper Example

One way we can strengthen the members is through our example. The Apostle Paul taught, "Be thou an example of the believers, in word, in conversation, in charity, in spirit, in faith, in purity" (1 Timothy 4:12). Our lives will influence others no matter where we are or what we are doing. It is important that we be good examples of righteousness at all times and in all places.

### Be a Good Home Teacher

▪ Show visual 6-a, "Home teaching is an important duty of the teacher."

We can magnify our callings to teach and strengthen the members by home teaching. In performing this duty, we should remember that we are entitled to the inspiration of the Lord. The Lord has said that all those who are ordained to preach the gospel are to do so by "the Spirit, even the Comforter which was sent forth to teach the truth" (see D&C 50:13–14).

▪ How can we know what to teach the families we are assigned to teach?

The following story shows how a teacher learned about the importance of home teaching.

"My legs felt shaky and there was an odd feeling in the pit of my stomach as we approached the door. I was sure that I was going to faint as my companion told me that this was 'my' door.

"No, I wasn't a new missionary. I was a fifteen-year-old home teacher climbing the stairs to the apartment of Sister Rice, a widow living in our ward. . . .

"[My companion] Brother Gabbott had given me a topic to present to the five families assigned us. I was prepared with some notes on a paper, but I was frightened and inexperienced. . . .

"We knocked on the door, but there was no immediate response. I was about to suggest that no one was home when the door slowly opened. From behind it appeared the frail figure of an aged sister, uncertain of what she'd find at her door. She smiled as she recognized Brother Gabbott. We were invited in and asked to take a seat.

"After a short greeting, Brother Gabbott looked at me as if to say, 'Okay, Robert, it's time to give our message.' The feeling in my stomach got worse as I began to speak. I cannot recall what I said, but as I looked up from my notes, I saw the tear-stained cheeks of that sweet, sensitive sister. She expressed her gratitude for the presence of priesthood bearers in her home.

*6-a, Home teaching is an important duty of the teacher.*

"I was speechless. What had I done? What could I do? Fortunately, Brother Gabbott helped me by bearing his testimony and asking if there were any needs in the home. There were.

"Sister Rice said that she had not been feeling well and asked that she be remembered as we offered our prayer before leaving. She then turned to me and asked if I would offer that prayer. . . .

"I consented and offered a benediction upon that home teaching visit, asking that a special blessing of health and strength be given to that faithful sister whom I barely knew but quickly came to love and respect.

"Twenty-five years have passed since my introduction to home teaching in Sister Rice's home, and she has long since died. But I cannot pass that house without thinking about the experience provided by Brother Gabbott and a faithful sister who knew the appropriateness of calling upon an obedient high priest and an insecure, frightened teacher in the Aaronic Priesthood" (Robert F. Jex, "My First Door," *Tambuli*, Dec. 1989, 45).

Like this home teacher, we can strengthen our assigned home teaching families by praying with them, encouraging them to do their family duties, and helping them to live the gospel. If the families we teach need help, we should report their needs to our priesthood authorities.

When we visit our assigned families, we must remember that we do so with the permission of the heads of these families. Because they are responsible to the Lord for their families, we should always teach their families under their direction. Only by teaching under the direction of the heads of the families can we fulfill our duties as teachers.

When we do our home teaching the way the Lord wants us to do it, we are building love and unity in the Church. The following story is a good example of what can happen when we take our callings as teachers seriously:

"Recently . . . a man and his teacher-age son were assigned to our family as home teachers. We knew of the father's dedication to the gospel but did not know what to expect from his son, although the young man's appearance and conduct seemed to reflect the same dedication. During their first visit with us, I kept my eye on this young man. Though reasonably quiet, everything that he did or said brought dignity to the priesthood he bore. Soon they learned that our young son had passed away a year ago and that we were expecting another child. From that moment on they were a special part of our lives as they prayed for and encouraged us. At the conclusion of that first visit I asked the young man to offer a prayer. In his prayer he asked the Lord to sustain us in the loss of our son and to bless the child that soon would be born. He specifically prayed that my wife would have no difficulty in delivering the baby. My wife and I were overcome by the sincerity and sensitivity of this young teacher. During the days and weeks that followed these brethren inquired about us regularly (more often than once a month). Following the birth of the baby, the young man, with his father, brought a gift. As we all knelt in prayer the teacher expressed his gratitude to the Lord for the safe delivery of the child" (as retold by H. Burke Peterson in "The Role of the Teacher," *New Era,* May 1974, 10–11).

- What can we do to be better home teachers?

### Greet the Members at Church

We can magnify our calling to be a good example by greeting the members as they come to the meetinghouse. We can shake their hands and ask about their well-being. When we usher at the door with this kind of warm, friendly feeling, we are helping to increase the love and unity among the members.

### Prepare the Sacrament

The Savior taught that true service is to do something without expecting praise for doing it. Preparing the sacrament is a good example of this principle. Members often do not realize that the teachers prepare the sacrament, for it is often prepared without any recognition being given to those who prepared it. But the service is performed nevertheless, and the Lord is pleased because it is true service.

- What can we do to prepare ourselves both physically and spiritually to prepare the sacrament? (Include the idea of being physically clean.)

### Help at Home

As teachers we can also help our own families. It is important to help clean and repair the house, take care of the yard, or do other work as needed. Also, as priesthood holders we can help our families live the gospel.

- Show visual 6-b, "An Aaronic Priesthood holder who magnifies his priesthood callings helps strengthen his family."

An inactive priesthood holder had not taken the necessary steps to have his wife and teenage son sealed to him in the temple. His son became deeply interested in eternal family unity after hearing a lesson

*6-b, An Aaronic Priesthood holder who magnifies his priesthood callings helps strengthen his family.*

in priesthood meeting about temple marriage. The lesson influenced the boy to talk to his father concerning the matter. As a result of their conversation, the father's life changed. He realized that he loved his wife and son and wanted to be with them forever. Eventually, the family was sealed in the temple for time and eternity—all because one family member, a teacher, was interested in building love and unity in his family.

### Be a Peacemaker

We can fulfill our responsibilities as teachers by being peacemakers in our families and in the Church. One way to do this is to look for the good in others. As we look for the good in others, we will strengthen their self-esteem. Other ways are to avoid gossip or rumors that would injure another person's reputation and to always use love and kindness in dealing with others. As we develop these tools and use them, we will be able to help many people experience peace in their lives.

### Conclusion

As teachers, we should always try to strengthen the Church, promote unity and love, and help members do their duties. Even though we may be young or new converts to the Church, we have the power to influence others for good. We should always remember that the Lord gives no commandments to us, "save he shall prepare a way for [us to] accomplish the thing which he commandeth" (1 Nephi 3:7).

- Plan with the class a specific service project that you could do to help build unity and love in your Church unit.

### Challenges

Prayerfully consider the needs of the families you home teach.

Prepare a message suited to the needs of each family as directed by the Spirit.

Visit your assigned families with your home teaching companion early each month.

Pray with your assigned families.

Perform those services you can perform which are needed by your assigned families. Communicate those you cannot perform to your quorum leaders.

### Additional Scripture

- Jacob 1:17–19 (how teachers should magnify their priesthood callings)

**Teacher Preparation**

Before presenting this lesson:

1. Read Doctrine and Covenants 20:53–60 and lesson 4, "The Priesthood Quorum," in this manual.

2. Assign class members to present any stories, scriptures, or quotations you wish.

# DUTIES OF THE PRIEST

*L e s s o n    7*

---

The purpose of this lesson is to help us understand the duties of priests.

## Introduction

The Lord commanded every priesthood holder to "stand in his own office, and labor in his own calling" (D&C 84:109). To do this, we must first learn and then fulfill our different responsibilities in the priesthood. As priests, we have all the responsibilities and duties of a deacon and teacher. In addition, our duties include teaching, baptizing, administering the sacrament, visiting the members, ordaining others to the Aaronic Priesthood, and assisting in missionary work. As we perform these duties, we are not only helping to build the kingdom of God but also preparing ourselves to receive the Melchizedek Priesthood. When we receive the Melchizedek Priesthood and are ordained to the office of elder, we can be called to serve full-time missions. Our effectiveness as full-time missionaries depends on how well prepared we are to serve. We can prepare to be good missionaries by magnifying our callings as priests.

## The Duties of the Priest

Worthy brethren may be ordained priests when they are at least 16 years old. The specific duties of a priest are found in the Doctrine and Covenants.

- Ask the class members to read and mark Doctrine and Covenants 20:46–48. What are the duties of a priest?

- Display a poster of the following duties, or write the information on the chalkboard:

*7-a, A priest may baptize when authorized by the bishop or branch president.*

Duties of a Priest

1. Teach the gospel.
2. Baptize.
3. Administer the sacrament.
4. Visit the members.
5. Ordain others to the Aaronic Priesthood.
6. Assist in missionary work.

*Teach the Gospel*

One of our duties as priests is to "preach, teach, expound, exhort" (D&C 20:46). This means that we are to teach others the principles of the gospel. In order to teach the principles of the gospel, we must first learn what they are. The Lord said, "Seek not to declare my word, but first seek to obtain my word, and then shall your tongue be loosed; then, if you desire, you shall have my Spirit and my word, yea, the power of God unto the convincing of men" (D&C 11:21).

We obtain the word of God in several ways. We obtain it in our homes from our parents, in our priesthood quorums from those who instruct us, in Sunday School, in sacrament meeting, and in seminary and institute classes.

One of the best ways to learn the word of God is through daily, personal study of the scriptures. Every priesthood holder should set aside time to regularly study the scriptures. As we search and ponder the scriptures, the Lord will help us understand them. As we build our knowledge of the gospel, we can teach it to others.

We may also fulfill our duty to teach others the gospel through our righteous example. Many times our good example encourages others to live the gospel.

- What specific things can we do to teach the gospel?

*Baptize*

- Show visual 7-a, "A priest may baptize when authorized by the bishop or branch president."

Another duty priests have is to baptize (see D&C 20:46). Baptism by the proper authority is one of the most important and sacred ordinances in the Church, for it is the ordinance by which we become members of the Church, are forgiven of our sins, and enter the path to

*7-b, Priests have the sacred responsibility of administering
the sacrament to the members of the Church.*

the celestial kingdom. It is a priest's sacred responsibility to administer this saving ordinance when authorized to do so by the bishop or branch president.

### Administer the Sacrament

- Show visual 7-b, "Priests have the sacred responsibility of administering the sacrament to the members of the Church."

The honor of administering the sacrament is given mainly to the priests, who offer the sacramental prayers. As priests, we should be familiar with the sacramental prayers, dress appropriately, and wash our hands before performing this ordinance. Above all, we should be worthy to perform this sacred ordinance as the Savior's representatives.

### Visit the Members

The Lord has commanded priests to "visit the house of each member, and exhort them to pray vocally and in secret and attend to all family duties" (D&C 20:47). We can accomplish this as we home teach our assigned families. During these visits, we can find out the needs of the family members. We can pray with them. We can teach them the principles of the gospel and encourage them to attend to their family duties. We can be friendly to the family members at our Church meetings and in the neighborhood. And we can participate with them in Church, school, and community activities.

### Ordain Others to the Aaronic Priesthood

Priests also have the authority to ordain other priests, teachers, and deacons (see D&C 20:48), but only when authorized by the bishop or branch president. This power to confer the Aaronic Priesthood is sacred. It was restored to the earth by John the Baptist when he ordained Joseph Smith and Oliver Cowdery to the Aaronic Priesthood (see D&C 13). John the Baptist himself was given authority by an angel acting in the name of God (see D&C 84:28). The power to ordain others comes to us, therefore, from God. To perform this important ordinance, we should be worthy and have the Holy Ghost with us. (For further information see lesson 3, "The Restoration of the Priesthood," in this manual.)

### Assist in Missionary Work

- Show visual 7-c, "Assisting the full-time missionaries is both an obligation and an honor."

The calling of a priest also includes assisting in missionary work. This calling was part of the ancient Church. Members of the Aaronic Priesthood today are also to help the elders with their missions. Their

*7-c, Assisting the full-time missionaries is both an obligation and an honor.*

specific duty is to make appointments and prepare the way for the elders. (See D&C 84:107–8.) We can assist in missionary work by helping the full-time missionaries in our areas find families to teach and by making appointments for them with these families. We can also assist in missionary work by preparing ourselves to be full-time missionaries.

**Magnifying Priesthood Callings**

As priests we should study our duties to teach, baptize, administer the sacrament, visit the members, ordain others, and assist in missionary work. As we learn and perform these duties, we are entitled to the protection and guidance of the Lord. President Wilford Woodruff, who served on a mission as a priest with an elder as his companion, said this about his mission:

"I went out as a Priest, and my companion as an Elder, and we traveled thousands of miles, and had many things manifested to us. I desire to impress upon you the fact that it does not make any difference whether a man is a Priest or an Apostle, if he magnifies his calling. A Priest holds the keys of the ministering of angels. Never in my life, as an Apostle, as a Seventy, or as an Elder, have I ever had more of the protection of the Lord than while holding the office of a Priest. The Lord revealed to me by visions, by revelations, and by the Holy Spirit, many things that lay before me" (*Millennial Star,* 5 Oct. 1891, 629).

Bishop Victor L. Brown related the following experience about how priests should magnify their callings:

"A young man . . . wrote the following: 'At one time I attended a ward which had almost no Melchizedek Priesthood holders in it. But it was not in any way dulled in spirituality. On the contrary, many of its members witnessed the greatest display of priesthood power they had ever known.

" 'The power was centered in the priests. For the first time in their lives they were called upon to perform all the duties of the priests and administer to the needs of their fellow ward members. They were seriously called to home teach—not just to be a yawning appendage to an elder making a social call but to bless their brothers and sisters.

" 'Previous to this time I had been with four of these priests in a different situation. There I regarded them to be common hoodlums. They drove away every seminary teacher after two or three months. They spread havoc over the countryside on Scouting trips. *But when they were needed—when they were trusted with a vital mission—they were among those who shone the most brilliantly in priesthood service.*

" 'The secret was that the bishop called upon his Aaronic Priesthood to rise to the stature of men to whom angels might well appear; and they rose to that stature, administering relief to those who might be in want and strengthening those who needed strengthening. Not only were the other ward members built up but so were the members of the quorum themselves. A great unity spread throughout the ward and every member began to have a taste of what it is for a people to be of one mind and one heart. There was nothing inexplicable in all of this; it was just the proper exercise of the Aaronic Priesthood' " (in Conference Report, Oct. 1975, 101–2; or *Ensign,* Nov. 1975, 68).

- Ask class members to share rewarding experiences they have had in magnifying their priesthood duties.

### Preparing to Be Effective Missionaries

One of the purposes of the Aaronic Priesthood is to prepare those who hold it to receive the Melchizedek Priesthood. Those priests who are worthy and who magnify the Aaronic Priesthood can receive the Melchizedek Priesthood and be ordained to the office of elder.

Much of full-time missionary work is accomplished today by elders. Most of us who now hold the Aaronic Priesthood worthily will be ordained elders at the age of 18. This gives us one year to learn and practice the duties of an elder and to prepare to serve a full-time mission.

If we perform all our duties as priests, we will gain experience in the very things we will be doing as missionaries. We will teach the gospel as missionaries, baptize converts, administer the sacrament on occasion, visit members, and ordain others to the priesthood. As we perform these duties as priests, we will be strengthened spiritually and will be better prepared to serve as full-time missionaries when we are called.

- Why is it important for priests to prepare and plan for a mission?

### Conclusion

Speaking to members of the Aaronic Priesthood, Elder David B. Haight said: "The Aaronic Priesthood years are critical years of preparation. The Lord knew young men would need these valuable teen years to prepare for life—precious years with meaningful, never-to-be-forgotten spiritual experiences. You will face some crucial decisions, but hopefully you will take advantage of the seasoned experience and counsel of your loving parents and concerned priesthood leaders" (in Conference Report, Oct. 1991, 50; or *Ensign,* Nov. 1991, 36).

As priests we should use our years of preparation wisely. We should follow the counsel of our parents and priesthood leaders and diligently perform our priesthood duties. Our duties include teaching the gospel, baptizing, administering the sacrament, visiting the members, ordaining others to the Aaronic Priesthood, and doing missionary work. By fulfilling these priesthood duties, we can bless and serve others now and be better prepared to serve as Melchizedek Priesthood bearers and full-time missionaries.

## Challenges

Faithfully perform your Aaronic Priesthood duties in order to:

Strengthen the members of your quorum and ward or branch.

Prepare yourself to receive the Melchizedek Priesthood and serve as a full-time missionary.

## Teacher Preparation

Before presenting this lesson:

1. Read Doctrine and Covenants 20:46–49.

2. Prepare the poster suggested in the lesson, or write the information on the chalkboard.

3. Assign class members to present any stories, scriptures, or quotations you wish.

# DUTIES OF THE BISHOP AND THE BRANCH PRESIDENT

*Lesson 8*

The purpose of this lesson is to help us understand the responsibilities of bishops and branch presidents so we can know how to support and sustain them.

### Introduction

During the Savior's mortal ministry, He organized His Church on the earth. After His death, congregations of believers met together to worship, learn the gospel, and strengthen and serve each other. Today members of The Church of Jesus Christ of Latter-day Saints are also organized into congregations. The purpose of these congregations is to help all people "come unto Christ, and be perfected in him" (Moroni 10:32). Large congregations are called wards and are presided over by a bishop.

Small congregations are called branches and are presided over by a branch president. "A branch may be organized when at least two member families live in an area and one of the members is a worthy Melchizedek Priesthood holder or a worthy priest in the Aaronic Priesthood. The stake, mission, or district presidency organizes and supervises the branch" (*Branch Guidebook* [1993], 1). As it grows, a branch can develop into a ward.

### The Appointment of Bishops and Branch Presidents

A bishop is called by inspiration of the Lord and ordained by a stake president under the direction of the First Presidency of the Church and the Quorum of the Twelve. A ward bishopric consists of three high priests—a bishop and two counselors. The bishop is the presiding high priest and presides over all the members in his ward. In addition, he is the president of the priests quorum and, together with his counselors, is responsible to watch over and nurture the young men and young women in the ward.

Branch presidents are called by inspiration to be presiding authorities over their branches by the stake, mission, or district president. Branch presidents hold the Melchizedek Priesthood and serve with counselors. Their responsibilities are similar to those of the bishop. Scriptural references referring to bishops usually pertain to branch presidents also.

### The Temporal Responsibilities of Bishops and Branch Presidents

Temporal responsibilities are those duties having to do with the physical well-being of the ward or branch members.

One important temporal responsibility that a bishop or branch president has is to administer the Church welfare program in the ward or branch. Part of this responsibility includes administering fast offerings. Each fast Sunday members should fast for two consecutive meals and contribute a fast offering at least equal to the value of the food they would have eaten. (Those who are physically unable to fast need only contribute fast offerings.) As the Lord's representative, the bishop or branch president is accountable to the Lord for properly receiving, recording, and administering these offerings. The bishop or branch president knows the members of his ward or branch, and when they need help he can assist them by using the fast offerings or by calling on members of his ward for help. (See D&C 84:112.)

The following story shows how a bishop helped a family in need:

"Situated beneath the heavily traveled freeway which girds Salt Lake City is the home of a sixty-year-old single man who has, due to a crippling disease, never known a day without pain nor many days without loneliness. One winter's day as I visited him, he was slow in answering the doorbell's ring. I entered his well-kept home; the temperature in save but one room, the kitchen, was a chilly 40 degrees. The reason: not sufficient money to heat any other room. The walls needed papering, the ceilings to be lowered, the cupboards filled.

"Troubled by the experience of visiting my friend, a bishop was consulted and a miracle of love, prompted by testimony, took place. The ward members were organized and the labor of love begun. A month later, my friend Lou called and asked if I would come and see what had happened to him. I did, and indeed beheld a miracle. The sidewalks which had been uprooted by large poplar trees had been replaced, the porch of the home rebuilt, a new door with glistening hardware installed, the ceilings lowered, the walls papered, the woodwork painted, the roof replaced, and the cupboards filled. No longer was the home chilly and uninviting. It now seemed to whisper a warm welcome. Lou saved until last showing me his pride and joy: there on his bed was a beautiful plaid quilt bearing the crest of his McDonald family clan. It had been made with loving care by the women of the Relief Society. Before leaving, I discovered that each week the Young

Adults would bring in a hot dinner and share a home evening. Warmth had replaced the cold; repairs had transformed the wear of years; but more significantly, hope had dispelled despair and now love reigned triumphant" (Thomas S. Monson, in Conference Report, Oct. 1977, 11; or *Ensign,* Nov. 1977, 9).

Bishops and branch presidents have other temporal duties such as keeping records of all Church business and overseeing the use and security of Church buildings and facilities. They also conduct tithing settlement and receive other contributions from Church members such as funds to support missionaries.

### The Spiritual Responsibilities of Bishops and Branch Presidents

Bishops and branch presidents are called to care for the spiritual well-being of the members of their Church units. One specific spiritual responsibility that bishops and branch presidents have is to be a common judge (see D&C 107:74). As a common judge, the bishop or branch president conducts worthiness interviews, counsels members, and administers Church discipline. In order to help them in these duties, the Lord has promised bishops and branch presidents the gift of discernment (see D&C 46:27).

The gift of discernment enables a bishop or branch president to know truth, to understand the differences between good and evil, and even to know what is in a person's heart. Because he has this gift, we can seek his counsel and he can tell us what the Lord would have us do to grow spiritually.

Through the gift of discernment the bishop in the following story was able to help a young man in his ward:

Craig, a 16-year-old priest, was an outstanding young man. He was always willing and ready to do whatever he was asked to do by his bishop. One day, however, Bishop Wells noticed that Craig was avoiding him. Even in priesthood quorum meeting, Craig's eyes were always looking in another direction. Bishop Wells wanted to call Craig as secretary to the priests quorum, but he felt something was wrong. So he called Craig into his office for an interview. During the interview Craig confessed that he had a moral problem. He said he was ashamed and did not feel worthy of the priesthood. Bishop Wells talked with him and assured him that he could repent and feel good about himself again. Through this talk, Craig learned how to overcome his problem, and through repentance, he was forgiven and became happy and enthusiastic again. Bishop Wells was then able to call him to be the secretary of the priests quorum.

■ How did the bishop's use of the gift of discernment help Craig to grow spiritually?

Because the bishop or branch president is a common judge in Israel, we can confess our sins to him and he can help us repent. When members commit serious sins, the bishop or branch president has the responsibility for holding disciplinary councils. These disciplinary councils are conducted in love and are meant to help the individual repent and enjoy once more the blessings of the gospel. (See D&C 50.14, 17 18, 42–43.) Leaders must be guided and inspired by the Lord in these matters.

Some additional spiritual duties of bishops and branch presidents include the following:

Preside over ward meetings.

Conduct ward business.

Coordinate the work of the Melchizedek Priesthood.

Oversee callings and releases.

Oversee the performance of ordinances and blessings.

Recommend brethren for advancement to the Melchizedek Priesthood.

Give blessings of comfort and counsel.

Interview and recommend worthy members to serve as full-time missionaries.

### Supporting Our Priesthood Leaders

Our bishop or branch president has been called by the Lord. For this reason, it is important that we sustain him in his calling. Elder Boyd K. Packer said: "A man who says he will sustain the President of the Church or the General Authorities, but cannot sustain his own bishop is deceiving himself. The man who will not sustain the bishop of his ward and the president of his stake will not sustain the President of the Church" (*Follow the Brethren*, Brigham Young University Speeches of the Year, [23 Mar. 1965], 4–5).

Elder L. Tom Perry taught: "I promise you, my brothers and sisters, if we will sustain and support our bishops, learn to be concerned for their welfare, and pray for their success in all they have to do, it will bless our lives as we are placed under their leadership and have opportunity to follow their inspired direction, as they lead the wards of the Church" (in Conference Report, Oct. 1982, 43; or *Ensign*, Nov. 1982, 32). His counsel can also be applied to supporting our branch presidents.

The scriptures teach us some of the ways we can sustain our priesthood leaders.

- Ask class members to follow along as each of the following scriptures is read. After each scripture is read, ask the class members to explain what it tells us we can do to support our leaders.

| SCRIPTURE | COUNSEL |
|---|---|
| Doctrine and Covenants 6:9 | Teach repentance and live the commandments. |
| 1 Nephi 3:7 | Accept and fulfill all callings that are given to us. |
| Doctrine and Covenants 60:2 | Share our talents. |
| Malachi 3:8–10 | Pay tithes and offerings. |
| Hebrews 13:17 | Be obedient to the counsel of our leaders. |
| Doctrine and Covenants 64:9–10 | Be forgiving of the weaknesses of others, including those of our leaders. |

The success that our bishop or branch president has in his calling is largely determined by how we sustain him. We should always pray that Heavenly Father will guide him to lead us in the right way.

**Conclusion**

The service performed by bishops and branch presidents is vital to our well-being. Worthy men called to serve as bishops and branch presidents are called to give direction to the members of the Church. They serve and love us, and we should do all we can to help them accomplish their duties. As we support them, we will find that we are blessed by their leadership.

**Challenges**

Pray for your Church leaders in your personal and family prayers.

Refrain from criticizing or gossiping about your Church leaders.

Sustain your Church leaders by following their righteous counsel.

**Additional Scriptures**

- 1 Timothy 3:1–7 (the qualifications of bishops)
- Titus 1:5–9 (the qualifications of bishops)

## Teacher Preparation

Before presenting this lesson:

1. Invite the bishop or branch president to attend the class so that he can answer any questions class members may have about his calling.

2. Assign class members to present any stories, scriptures, or quotations you wish.

# DUTIES OF THE ELDER AND THE HIGH PRIEST

*Lesson 9*

The purpose of this lesson is to help us understand the duties of elders and high priests.

## Introduction

As we learn our priesthood duties and fulfill them, we bless the lives of others because we are the representatives of the Savior. He has given us His priesthood so that, by performing our duties, we can help those we serve progress toward eternal life. This is especially true for those of us who hold the Melchizedek Priesthood because this priesthood holds "the keys of all the spiritual blessings of the church" (D&C 107:18). Those of us who have received the Melchizedek Priesthood have been ordained to the office of elder or high priest within this priesthood. Each of these offices has its special duties, but many of the responsibilities are the same.

## The Responsibilities of the Melchizedek Priesthood

By being faithful in our responsibilities as Aaronic Priesthood holders, we prepare ourselves to receive the Melchizedek Priesthood. When the time approaches for our ordination to the Melchizedek Priesthood, we are interviewed by those in authority. One Aaronic Priesthood holder wrote the following account of what he thought and felt after his interview to be advanced to the Melchizedek Priesthood:

"The Stake President looked deep into my eyes as he asked me his last question and listened to my response. He then said, 'George, I feel you are ready and worthy to be given the Melchizedek Priesthood and be ordained an Elder.' A few moments later I was walking through the dark night air. . . . I've never been more calmly excited. . . . Soon I knelt at my bed. I decided I'd do all I could to use my priesthood with honor. I decided I'd never swear, or tell a dirty story, or hurt anyone. I decided I'd really try to be a man of God. I'll always remember that night. That was really the beginning of everything. It was so good to be called to hold the priesthood. It's so good now to strive with all my heart to be chosen as one worthy to use that priesthood; to be a blessing to my family . . . and to my fellowman" (George D. Durrant, *Kentucky Louisville Mission Newsletter*, Oct. 19, 1974).

▪ What commitment did this young man make after his interview? What are some commitments we should make when we become Melchizedek Priesthood holders?

We should all strive to learn our duties and to be worthy to use the priesthood (see D&C 107:99–100). As Melchizedek Priesthood holders, we all have certain responsibilities no matter what office we hold.

▪ Show visual 9-a, "Priesthood authority is conferred through the laying on of hands by those who have been given authority of God."

The following are some responsibilities of the Melchizedek Priesthood:

### Personal Conversion

We should be personally converted to the gospel of Jesus Christ and be thoroughly committed to living its principles.

### Home and Family Relations

We should teach our families the principles of the gospel and treat them with love and understanding.

### Family History and Temple Work

We should be worthy to hold a temple recommend, obtain the blessings of the temple for ourselves and our families, find the names of our ancestors, and perform temple ordinances for them. We should promote "[the turning of] the heart of the fathers to the children, and the heart of the children to their fathers" by keeping family records (such as personal journals, family group records, and family histories) and by maintaining family organizations (see D&C 128:17–18).

### Welfare Services

We should provide for ourselves and our families and help those in need through the welfare program of the Church.

### Missionary Work

We should engage in appropriate missionary activities, such as helping family members prepare for and serve full-time missions, friendshipping nonmembers, providing referrals for the missionaries, serving full-time missions, and financially supporting missionary work.

### Home Teaching

We should understand our full responsibilities as home teachers and diligently "watch over . . . and be with and strengthen" those we are called to serve (see D&C 20:53).

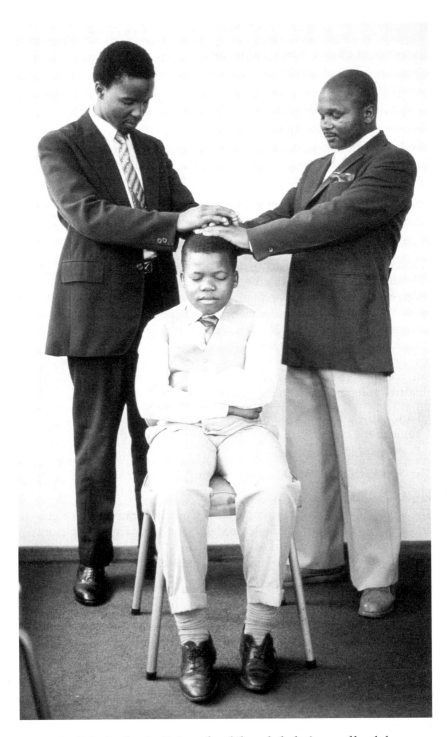

*9-a, Priesthood authority is conferred through the laying on of hands by those who have been given authority of God.*

### Quorum and Church Participation and Service

We should serve diligently in our Church callings, perform other Church and quorum duties, and participate in appropriate Church meetings and activities, thereby building the kingdom of God.

### Community Participation and Service

We should "honor, obey, and sustain the law; be loyal citizens and good neighbors; and improve the community in which [we] live" (*Annual Guidelines, 1978–79: The Melchizedek Priesthood* [1978], 1).

- Show visual 9-b, "A father's blessing is one way to bless the spiritual lives of others."

### Ordinances

When we are given the Melchizedek Priesthood, we are given the power to bless the spiritual lives of others. The Melchizedek Priesthood "administereth the gospel and holdeth the key . . . of the knowledge of God. Therefore, in the ordinances thereof, the power of godliness is manifest" (see D&C 84:19–21). Through the power of the Melchizedek Priesthood, we can consecrate oil, bless the sick, confer the priesthood and the gift of the Holy Ghost, ordain others to priesthood offices, dedicate graves, give blessings of comfort, bestow father's blessings on our children, and participate in the higher temple ordinances.

- How is the power of God manifest in these ordinances? What are some of the blessings that you have received from the Melchizedek Priesthood?

### The Specific Duties of Elders and High Priests

#### Elder

The word *elder* has two meanings in the Church. It can refer in a general way to a holder of the Melchizedek Priesthood. For example, missionaries and many General Authorities have the title of *Elder*. *Elder* also refers to a specific office in the Melchizedek Priesthood.

- Ask class members to read Doctrine and Covenants 20:38–45, 42:44, 46:2, and 107:11–12. What are some of the responsibilities of the office of elder mentioned in these scriptures?

In addition to the responsibilities mentioned in these scriptures, elders are to officiate in any calling that may be required of them. President Joseph F. Smith explained that elders may be asked to work in the temples, labor in the ministry at home, and assist in preaching the gospel to the world (see *Gospel Doctrine*, 5th ed. [1939], 184–85).

#### High Priest

The rights and responsibilities of high priests are to preside and to hold all the authority of elders (see D&C 107:10). The calling to preside

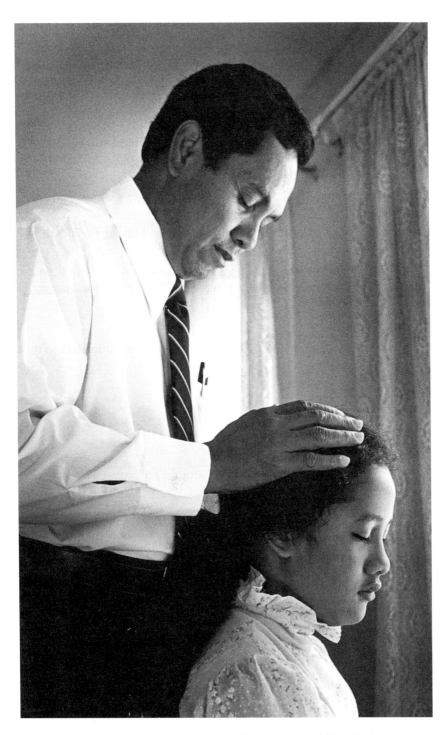

*9-b, A father's blessing is one way to bless the spiritual lives of others.*

includes, among others, the offices of General Authority, mission president, stake president, and bishop. As high priests preside in their various callings, they have the power to administer the spiritual blessings of their particular calling.

### Conclusion

The Melchizedek Priesthood holds the keys of all the spiritual blessings of the Church. Therefore, when we officiate in our priesthood offices as elders and high priests, we can bless both the spiritual and temporal lives of those we serve.

### Challenges

Identify the duties of your office in the priesthood and make a plan to better fulfill them.

Identify a specific need in your own home. Decide on a way to become a better father or family member by righteously exercising the priesthood in your home.

### Additional Scripture

- Doctrine and Covenants 124:137 (elders are standing ministers to the Church)

---

### Teacher Preparation

Before presenting this lesson:

1. Read Doctrine and Covenants 107.

2. Assign class members to present any stories, scriptures, or quotations you wish.

# PATRIARCHS AND PATRIARCHAL BLESSINGS

*Lesson 1 0*

The purpose of this lesson is to help us understand the role of patriarchs and to prepare us to receive a patriarchal blessing.

## Introduction

The Lord loves all His children and desires to bless them. Our actions and choices, however, determine the extent to which He can bless us. President Joseph F. Smith said: "Every person will receive his just reward for the good he may do and for his every act. But let it be remembered that all blessings which we shall receive, either here or hereafter, must come to us as a result of our obedience to the laws of God upon which these blessing are predicated" ("What is to Become of Such as Me?" *Improvement Era*, Nov. 1912, 71).

When we receive our patriarchal blessings, we are told many of the blessings Heavenly Father has in store for us in this world and in eternity. These blessings will be ours if we live true and faithful lives. Knowing these things in advance can motivate us to be worthy to receive the blessings promised to us.

## What Is a Patriarch?

Patriarchs are fathers. Adam was the first patriarch, and he was responsible for blessing his posterity and helping them live righteously. One of the last acts of service Adam performed for his children was to give them a patriarchal blessing.

- Have class members read Doctrine and Covenants 107:53–57.

In a vision Joseph Smith saw Adam calling his children together and giving them patriarchal blessings. Then he saw the Lord appear to them, and Adam foretold what should happen to his family. Speaking of this great event, the Prophet Joseph Smith said, "This is why Adam blessed his posterity; he wanted to bring them into the presence of God" (see *Teachings of the Prophet Joseph Smith*, sel. Joseph Fielding Smith [1976], 158–59).

The word *patriarch* is also the title of an office in the Melchizedek Priesthood. In the organization of the Church in Jesus' time, patriarchs were called evangelists (see Ephesians 4:11). When the Church was restored, this priesthood office was also restored. Joseph Smith explained that "an Evangelist is a Patriarch. . . . Wherever the Church of Christ is established in the earth, there should be a Patriarch for the benefit of the posterity of the Saints" (*Teachings of the Prophet Joseph Smith*, 151).

Most stakes of the Church have one worthy Melchizedek Priesthood bearer who is called and ordained under the direction of the Quorum of the Twelve to be the stake patriarch. As a high priest, he has the authority to perform any duty a high priest can perform; but because he is a patriarch, he also has the specific responsibility to bestow blessings on members of the stake who seek patriarchal blessings.

Patriarchs have the right and are inspired to give patriarchal blessings in the name of the Lord. These blessings can bring comfort in hours of sorrow or trouble, can strengthen faith, and can help motivate us to live worthy of the blessings the Lord has in store for us. (See Joseph Fielding Smith, *Doctrines of Salvation*, comp. Bruce R. McConkie, 3 vols. [1954–56], 3:170.)

**What Is a Patriarchal Blessing?**

- Show visual 10-a, "Patriarchal blessings reveal lineage and promise blessings that can be obtained through righteous living."

In 1957 the First Presidency of the Church explained that a patriarchal blessing contains an inspired declaration of lineage. We are also given inspired and prophetic directions and promises about our missions in life. These blessings include promises of spiritual gifts, temporal blessings, advice, and warnings that will help us accomplish our life missions. (See First Presidency letter to stake presidents, 28 June 1957.)

One important part of a patriarchal blessing is the declaration of our lineage, which tells us through which tribe of Israel we receive our blessings. Because of our ancestry, we are entitled to receive, according to our righteousness, the same blessings given to Adam, Abraham, Jacob, and other great prophets of God. (See Eldred G. Smith, in Conference Report, Apr. 1971, 145–47; or *Ensign*, June 1971, 100–101.)

When we joined The Church of Jesus Christ of Latter-day Saints we became heirs of Heavenly Father. This means that we will receive all the blessings that Heavenly Father has for us—if we live righteous lives. These are the same blessings promised to Abraham. Members of the Church are either directly descended from Abraham or adopted into one of the tribes of Israel because they have accepted the true gospel. (See Romans 8:14–17; Galatians 3:26–29; D&C 63:20; 86:8–10.)

Another important part of a patriarchal blessing is the insight given us about our missions while in this life. Through our patriarchal blessings, Heavenly Father tells us what our purposes are here on earth and how to accomplish them. The fulfillment of our blessings, however, is conditional.

Elder John A. Widtsoe taught that some of these blessings may not come in this life: "It should always be kept in mind that the realization of the promises made may come in this or the future life. Men have stumbled at times because promised blessings have not occurred in this life. They have failed to remember that, in the gospel, life with all its activities continues forever and that the labors of the earth may be continued in heaven" (*Evidences and Reconciliations,* arr. G. Homer Durham, 3 vols. in 1 [1960], 323).

- Ask the assigned class member to share his testimony of the guidance and support his patriarchal blessing has been to him in his life.

**Receiving a Patriarchal Blessing**

To receive our patriarchal blessings, we must meet certain personal requirements. We must:

1. Be worthy, baptized members of the Church.

2. Have a desire to receive direction from the Lord.

3. Have studied the gospel and know the purpose of patriarchal blessings.

4. Be mature enough to appreciate the significance of and receive encouragement from the blessing.

5. Receive a recommend from our bishop or branch president.

6. Make an appointment with the stake patriarch to receive our patriarchal blessing.

Before we go to receive our blessing, we should pray to prepare ourselves spiritually, and we should pray for the patriarch that he may be inspired on our behalf. We may also fast to prepare ourselves.

- Ask the assigned class member to describe how he prepared to receive his patriarchal blessing.

When patriarchs give us our blessings, they record them. They do this so they can give us a printed copy of our blessing. A copy is also filed in the official records of the Church. This way, if any of us ever loses his blessing, he can get another copy of it from the Church.

Because a patriarchal blessing is personal and sacred, it should be kept in a safe but convenient place. Its content should be shared only with close

10-a, Patriarchal blessings reveal lineage and promise blessings that can be obtained through righteous living.

family members. In order for our patriarchal blessings to help us, we should study them often. As we do, we will know what we must do to receive the promised blessings.

## Conclusion

The following story shows how one person was blessed when he worked faithfully to follow the counsel given to him in one part of his patriarchal blessing.

"I had always felt that I had some purpose in life, and that I would accomplish a great mission, but I did not know how I was going to bring this to pass, for I reached my adult years without having learned to adequately read or write.

"I thought I was as smart as the other boys, but my scholastic record indicated otherwise—I was a straight *F* student. A special battery of school-administered tests, that were based on reading, indicated that I was not too bright—that perhaps I shouldn't even be walking around by myself. Very simple academic skills the other boys accomplished easily were too difficult for me. As a teenager, I was once asked by one of the other boys to spell the word *gas,* something I could not do. With a record of nothing but failure, I began to feel that I must actually be stupid, just as people had been implying for some time, and were now actually beginning to say about me.

"I 'graduated' from high school only because this seemed the simplest way for the school to rid itself of the problem of trying to educate a student they judged to be incapable of learning even the simple third-grade skills of reading.

"Strangely enough, my first contact with the truths of the restored gospel came when I was fourteen years old and attempted to read one of the books I found in the family bookcase. I had come across a Book of Mormon that belonged to my mother, who had been baptized a member of the Church in the rural south of Tennessee many years before. But, because of her isolation from other Church members, she was never taught much about the gospel and soon drifted away, so she was lacking in the knowledge and desire to teach her children the gospel contained within that Book of Mormon.

"I struggled through the testimony of Joseph Smith, reading only the simple words, and skipping the big words that I did not understand. It is not surprising that, at times, I read without any meaning at all, but for some reason a spirit came over me and I was convinced that what I was attempting to read was true. What I was able to read gave me a desire to know more about the Church, so that next Sunday morning, I hitchhiked across town to attend the Mormon Church.

This was the beginning of an eight-year period I spent in accumulating a testimony of the gospel, sufficient that I finally . . . entered the waters of baptism at the age of twenty-two.

"Now that I was a member of the Church and had embarked upon the path to celestial exaltation, I was no longer content with my lack of personal development and achievement. I wanted to grow as an individual in worth and usefulness in his kingdom, and to do this, there was much I had to learn, including learning how to read.

"I then did as we have always been counseled to do when making decisions and plans that will affect our eternal progress—I turned to the Lord for his guidance, and it was given to me in a patriarchal blessing in which I was told:

" 'You are choice in the eyes of God, as was Paul of old, a chosen servant who has been given the power and ability to accomplish a good work. Continue in your search for knowledge and pray for wisdom that you might glorify your Heavenly Father with your intelligence.'

"If the Lord thought I was capable of learning, then I *could* learn! But I realized that this blessing was not to be taken for granted, that it would not be fulfilled automatically, without further thought or action on my part. The fulfillment of this blessing, as it is with all patriarchal blessings, was predicated upon my worthiness and being willing to do those things necessary to bring those blessings about.

"I now had the faith that with the Lord's help I could learn if I would but apply myself, and this I did, studying from 6:00 A.M. until midnight, six days a week.

"I spent three hundred dollars on a set of records that contained the letters of the alphabet in basic terms. I spent night after night memorizing the alphabet, sounding out the letters, so that I could teach myself to read and write. I was still unable to spell very well, but I could read by breaking the words down phonetically until I understood them.

"Full of confidence in my new-found ability to read and spell, I enrolled in Ohio State University. I attempted to take notes as the professors lectured, but I was having difficulty in being able to spell the words sufficiently so that I could record them. I was still breaking nearly all my words down phonetically and, as a result, I was able to record only a small portion of the professors' lectures in my notes. And without accurate and complete notes it was impossible for me to study and adequately prepare for the examinations, so again, my academic attempts ended in failure, and I was forced to drop out of the University.

"I was discouraged and began to doubt my ability to achieve academically, but I had been given a blessing and a promise that I *could* learn.

So, realizing that the fulfillment of that promise rested solely upon my faith *and* works, I continued to work on my spelling and reading improvement.

"Taking the Lord at his word, that he would bless me if I did my part, I enrolled at Ricks College. I never missed completing my home teaching, and faithfully attended to all the responsibilities delegated to me by the Church—and studied eighteen hours a day. I still had to work at my reading, but I could now recognize words immediately, whereas before I had to break them down. When I went to take a test, I'd memorize *every* word in my notes, so I could spell them during the test. By the time I left Ricks, I could read well and was an honor student, graduating with a 3.6 grade-point average!

"I now hold a B.A. degree from Brigham Young University, having completed my desired studies with a 3.2 average.

"The promise of the Lord, 'that I had been given the ability to accomplish a good work' has been fulfilled, as will the other promises made to me in my patriarchal blessing, if I but have faith in him, and *work* to bring about the fulfillment of those blessings" (Dorvis Rodgers, "You Shall Glorify Your Father in Heaven with Your Intelligence," in Margie Calhoun Jensen, *When Faith Writes the Story* [1973], 34–37).

This person was prepared and obedient; as a result, his patriarchal blessing was a source of guidance and comfort to him. We should exercise the same faith in reaching for the blessings promised us in our patriarchal blessings.

### Challenges

Prepare yourself to receive your patriarchal blessing if you have not received it.

If you have received your blessing, read it frequently and strive to live worthy to receive the promised blessings.

### Additional Scriptures

- Genesis 49:1–28 (the patriarch Israel blesses his sons)

- Doctrine and Covenants 107:39–56 (the Twelve to ordain ministers; the patriarchal priesthood in ancient times)

- Doctrine and Covenants 124:91–92 (patriarchs receive keys to give blessings)

- Moses 6:1–6 (a book of remembrance kept to bless Adam's children)

**Teacher Preparation**

Before presenting this lesson:

1. Ask a member of the class who has received a patriarchal blessing to share his testimony of the guidance and blessing it has been in his life. (Caution him that a patriarchal blessing is personal and should not be read to others. For the same reason, he should not be very specific about the promises and instructions given him in the blessing.)

2. Assign another class member to tell what he did to prepare to receive his patriarchal blessing.

3. Assign class members to present any stories, scriptures, or quotations you wish.

# THE NEED FOR
# GENERAL AUTHORITIES

*L e s s o n   1 1*

The purpose of this lesson is to help us understand why the Lord calls General Authorities and how we are blessed by sustaining them.

**Introduction**

When the Savior lived on the earth, He organized His Church and ordained men to the priesthood. He called twelve Apostles and other men to bear testimony of Him and to help watch over the Church. After His death and Resurrection, He visited the Nephite people in America and organized His Church in the same way. He ordained twelve disciples to serve the Nephites in the same ways that the twelve Apostles served the Church in the Old World.

In these last days, the Lord has once again established the true Church of Jesus Christ through the Prophet Joseph Smith. It was organized by revelation and has twelve Apostles, just as the Church had when the Savior was on the earth. In addition to the Apostles, the Lord has called others to help lead and direct the entire Church. These men are called General Authorities.

- Show visual 11-a, "The First Presidency and Quorum of the Twelve Apostles of The Church of Jesus Christ of Latter-day Saints."

A General Authority is a Melchizedek Priesthood bearer called by the Lord to serve in one of the following positions:

*The First Presidency*

The First Presidency consists of the President of the Church and his counselors. The President holds all the keys and authority restored to the Church in the last days. Together with his counselors, the President watches over the whole Church and has power and authority to officiate in all the offices in the priesthood and in the Church.

The President of the Church has the keys of the priesthood to administer in all spiritual and temporal affairs of the Church. He has the right

# The First Presidency

President Thomas S. Monson
First Counselor

President Gordon B. Hinckley

President James E. Faust
Second Counselor

## The Quorum of the Twelve Apostles

Boyd K. Packer

L. Tom Perry

David B. Haight

Neal A. Maxwell

Russell M. Nelson

Dallin H. Oaks

M. Russell Ballard

Joseph B. Wirthlin

Richard G. Scott

Robert D. Hales

Jeffrey R. Holland

Henry B. Eyring

*11-a, The First Presidency and Quorum of the Twelve Apostles of
The Church of Jesus Christ of Latter-day Saints.*

to give to stake presidents, bishops, patriarchs, and others keys pertaining to specific offices in their geographical areas.

President Joseph F. Smith wrote that "every man ordained to any degree of the Priesthood, has this authority delegated to him. But it is necessary that every act performed under this authority shall be done at the proper time and place, in the proper way, and after the proper order. The power of directing these labors constitutes the *keys* of the priesthood" (*Gospel Doctrine*, 5th ed. [1939], 136).

### The Quorum of the Twelve Apostles

The Twelve Apostles are called by the Lord to be special witnesses of Jesus Christ. They act under the direction of the First Presidency.

### The Seventy

"The Seventy are to act in the name of the Lord, under the direction of the Twelve . . . , in building up the church and regulating all the affairs of the same in all nations" (D&C 107:34).

### The Presiding Bishopric

The Presiding Bishopric is the presidency of the Aaronic Priesthood working under the direction of the Quorum of the Twelve and the First Presidency. The Presiding Bishop and his two counselors watch over the physical, or temporal, affairs of the Church.

In addition to the General Authorities, a large number of men are called as Area Authority Seventies. They are not General Authorities, but are called to help build up the Church in specific areas of the world.

### Responsibilities of the General Authorities

The General Authorities are representatives of Jesus Christ. The Savior Himself is the head of the Church and directs it by revelation to the prophet and the other General Authorities. Through these men, the Lord reveals His will and teaches us everything that is necessary for our salvation.

General Authorities represent the Savior in many different ways:

1. They travel throughout the world to help and instruct Church members and local Church leaders.

2. They keep the Church unified and make sure that correct doctrines are taught.

3. They ordain local priesthood leaders, such as stake presidents and stake patriarchs.

4. They prepare and deliver talks at general conference and other meetings. When these men speak under the influence of the Holy Ghost,

it is the same as if Christ Himself were speaking. "What I the Lord have spoken, I have spoken . . . , whether by mine own voice or by the voice of my servants, it is the same" (D&C 1:38). By this means, they teach and inspire both Church members and nonmembers.

5. The Twelve have a calling to be special witnesses of Jesus Christ to all the world. They bear testimony of the divinity of Christ wherever they go. The other General Authorities also bear their testimonies of the Savior.

6. They have the responsibility for supervising all the administrative affairs of the Church.

7. Along with all of these duties, they are also fathers and husbands. Similar to other fathers in the Church, they have the responsibility to lead their own families and guide them to the celestial kingdom.

**Our Need for General Authorities**

Throughout history Heavenly Father has revealed His will to men on the earth through His prophets. This is true whether we are talking about the time of Noah, Moses, or Joseph Smith. Conditions may change, but the truth does not. Because of our continuing need for God's direction, He has given us a prophet and apostles and other General Authorities to guide us today.

The following story tells how a group of people were blessed by being obedient to a prophet:

"Finally in July 1959 the plans were completed. Thirty faithful Tahitians had worked, saved, and sacrificed to raise the money necessary to finance a trip to the Hawaii Temple. It had taken much work to bring the *Paraita* (literally the *Big Chief*), the mission yacht, into dry dock, to repair it, and to repaint it. Then there had been the problems with the French government. [The skipper, Brother Tapu, finally convinced the harbor master, and the two of them convinced the French governor to allow the Saints on the *Paraita* to sail for Hawaii.]

"Brother Tapu not only obtained permission from the French officials, but he also wrote to Salt Lake City to get permission from President David O. McKay. That permission had been granted and everything was ready.

"Then a fateful call came from the mission office. Everyone anticipating the voyage was to gather for a meeting at the mission home before departure. . . .

"That day a special messenger, Ernest C. Rossiter, . . . had arrived direct from President McKay in Salt Lake City. The news he brought was stunning. The Saints had been asked not to make their long-sought voyage. According to Brother Tapu, President McKay gave no explanation. He merely asked Brother Rossiter to 'go and stop them. They won't make it, and if we allow them to come, we'll be in trouble with the [French] government. We'll be responsible for them. So you go and stop them.'

"In the mission diary, President Christiansen [the mission president] wrote expressing his anxiety about telling the Saints who were ready to embark:

" 'I was much concerned and felt I needed the Lord's help to assist me in giving an explanation to these humble, faithful members, who had such high hopes of receiving their endowments in His Holy House. I fasted and prayed about it. I called a meeting of the priesthood members for July 15, 1959, at 8:00 o'clock, and also asked six of the faithful brethren to come to my room at 7:30, and with the help of President Rossiter we told them of the decision that had come from the First Presidency, and told them that we desired their faith and prayers in presenting the message to the members of the priesthood who would assemble at 8:00 o'clock. After President Rossiter and I had finished talking to these men, they in turn spoke briefly their thoughts, and as I listened a great joy swelled inside me as they told their desire to obey the counsel of our prophet here upon the earth.

" 'We went to the meeting with the priesthood members. After hearing the message from the First Presidency, [they] expressed their convictions that if this word had come from the leaders of the Church then it must have come through the inspiration of the Lord, and the only way to show their love and appreciation for the blessings He had given them was to be obedient to the counsel given. I then called for a vote, and all hands were raised accepting the decision of the First Presidency.'

"So the voyage was cancelled, and neither President Rossiter, nor President Christiansen, nor the faithful Tahitian Saints really knew why the prophet of God had told them not to go. They cancelled the voyage because they had faith in the prophet.

"Later, Brother Tapu, the skipper, returned to his boat where a mechanic told him that a small gear was damaged and would only provide 100 to 150 more hours of service. This fact notwithstanding, the boat was launched and anchored. . . .

" 'Well [reported Brother Tapu, the skipper of the boat], a couple of days later I got a call. I was over here at the mission office working on our local Church magazine. The call was from the harbor master. He said, "Hey, your boat's sinking." And I said, "What, I just got it out from dry dock!" He still said, "Your boat is sinking. Hurry!" So I rushed to the harbor and the boat was halfway down. My first mate was underneath the boat checking what was going on. He found that the exhaust pipe from the kitchen was rotten. The repairmen had painted over some very rotten wood and rusty pipe. It had broken and the water went in.

" 'So what would you say if we were two or three hundred miles away on a lifeboat? If we had sailed according to schedule, we would have been that far on our way when the rotten pipe and wood gave out.'

"At the time when the Saints in Tahiti had accepted the counsel of the prophet, they could not understand President McKay's reason for concern. But now they understood the ways of God. Brother Tapu expressed this knowledge when he said, 'That's why I always had a testimony of President McKay, a true prophet of the Lord' " (R. Lanier and JoAnn M. Britsch, "A Prophet's Warning," *New Era,* Mar. 1976, 12, 14).

The General Authorities speak for Christ. The Lord has said that "whatsoever they shall speak when moved upon by the Holy Ghost shall be scripture, shall be the will of the Lord, shall be the mind of the Lord, shall be the word of the Lord, shall be the voice of the Lord, and the power of God unto salvation" (D&C 68:4).

Because these men are the Savior's representatives on the earth, it is important that we know what they say and follow their teachings. General Authorities have emphasized many important teachings from the Lord in our time: They have counseled us to hold family home evening. They have asked us to help build temples and do our family history work. They have taught us about personal and family preparedness (including food storage). They have expressed the need for every member to do missionary work.

- Ask class members to think about how the world has changed in the last 10 or 20 years. How does listening to the prophets help us meet the challenges we face today?

### Sustaining the General Authorities

The Lord will not force any of us to obey His servants. We can either accept or reject them. It is a great blessing, however, to be able to accept and sustain the General Authorities and our other leaders. This we do formally at certain meetings in which we are asked to give our sustaining vote for the leadership of the Church. We show our willingness to sustain them by raising our right hand. But to sustain the General Authorities requires more than simply raising our right hand. We truly sustain the General Authorities by accepting their teachings and following their counsel and leadership.

These men are the representatives of Jesus Christ and receive continuing revelation from Him. We honor the Savior by honoring His representatives. We honor and respect our living prophets by obeying their teachings, praying for them, and praying for the strength to follow them. (See Hebrews 13:17–18 and D&C 107:22.) We also sustain them when we sustain our bishop or branch president, for he acts under their direction.

Great blessings come to those who sustain the General Authorities. The Lord has said that those who believe in the teachings of the prophets and endure in faith to the end will receive all that God has (see D&C 84:36–38). The Book of Mormon tells of a great man named Amulek who received a prophet of God. An angel visited Amulek and told him that the prophet Alma was going to visit him. The angel said: "Thou shalt receive him into thy house and feed him, and he shall bless thee and thy house; and the blessing of the Lord shall rest upon thee and thy house" (Alma 10:7). Amulek received Alma into his home and later bore his testimony of the great blessings that came to him and his family because he received the prophet.

▪ Read Alma 10:10–11. How can we receive the blessings described by Amulek?

We may never have a General Authority visit our home, but we can receive similar blessings if we accept the General Authorities by following their inspired counsel in our homes.

▪ Ask class members to share any experiences they have had when listening to a General Authority speak or reading his words. Why is it important to follow the counsel of the General Authorities?

**Conclusion**

The General Authorities are representatives of the Savior. They hold the priesthood and the keys to direct the work of the Lord's Church. As we follow their counsel and sustain them with our faith, obedience, and prayers, we will receive great blessings.

President Harold B. Lee taught: "Someone has said . . . and I believe it to be absolutely true: '[A] person is not truly converted until he sees the power of God resting upon the leaders of this church, and until it goes down into his heart like fire.' Until the members of this church have that conviction that they are being led in the right way, and they have a conviction that these men of God are men who are inspired and have been properly appointed by the hand of God, they are not truly converted" (in Conference Report, Apr. 1972, 118; or *Ensign*, July 1972, 103).

Conclude by having class members sing "We Thank Thee, O God, for a Prophet" (*Hymns*, no. 19; or *Gospel Principles*, 344).

## Challenges

In your family prayers and personal prayers, ask the Lord to bless the General Authorities.

Pray for a testimony and the strength to follow the prophet and the other General Authorities.

## Additional Scriptures

- Numbers 12:6 (the Lord appears to His prophets)

- Amos 3:7 (the Lord reveals His secrets to His prophets)

- Luke 1:59–79 (the Lord has always spoken to man through prophets)

- Doctrine and Covenants 21:4–6 (the prophet speaks words as if from the mouth of God)

- Doctrine and Covenants 43:1–7 (revelations for the Church given only through the prophet)

## Teacher Preparation

Before presenting this lesson, assign class members to present any stories, scriptures, or quotations you wish.

# PERSONAL
# AND FAMILY
# RESPONSIBILITIES

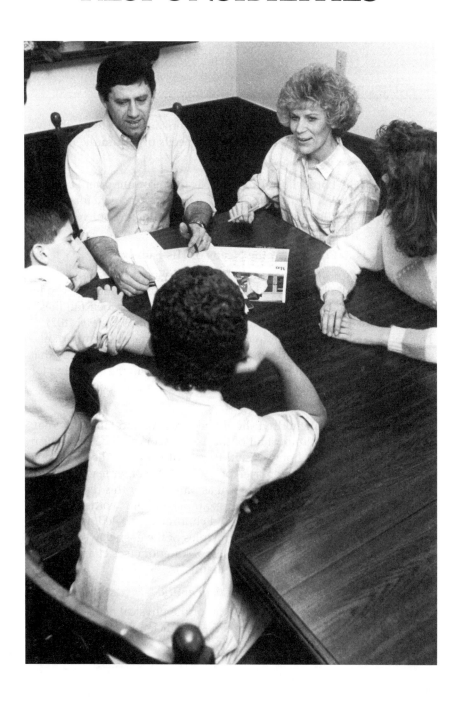

# THE FATHER'S RESPONSIBILITY FOR THE WELFARE OF HIS FAMILY

*L e s s o n   1 2*

---

The purpose of this lesson is to help us understand the responsibility the father has to plan and provide for the needs of his family.

**Introduction**

A prophet of the Lord said: "The family is the most important organization in time or in eternity. Our purpose in life is to create for ourselves eternal family units" (Joseph Fielding Smith, in Conference Report, Apr. 1972, 13; or *Ensign,* July 1972, 27).

**The Father Is to Provide for the Needs of His Family**

Prophets and Apostles have taught that "by divine design, fathers are to preside over their families in love and righteousness and are responsible to provide the necessities of life and protection for their families" ("The Family: A Proclamation to the World," *Ensign,* Nov. 1995, 102). This sacred obligation, given to us by the Lord, is the most important work a father will ever perform. President David O. McKay stated that "no other success can compensate for failure in the home" (quoting J. E. McCulloch, *Home: The Savior of Civilization* [1924], 42, in Conference Report, Apr. 1935, 116).

It is in the family that children should be cared for and taught eternal principles. "The most important of the Lord's work will be that which we do within our own homes," said President Harold B. Lee (Regional Representatives Seminar Report, Apr. 1972, 2). No other teacher can affect our children as much as we can as parents. For this reason, we must teach our children both by our example and our words. We are promised that if we and our wives and children are sealed together in the temple and faithfully live the principles of the gospel, we can live together as eternal families in the celestial kingdom (see chapter 47, "Exaltation," in the *Gospel Principles* manual).

*Providing for the Physical Needs of the Family*

As fathers, we are expected to provide for the physical needs of our families. To meet the physical necessities of our family we should:

1. Work at an honest job.

2. Budget family resources in cooperation with our wife.

3. Teach our children to work.

4. Direct a program of home production and storage.

Modern scriptures teach that those who could work but do not "shall not eat the bread nor wear the garments of the laborer" (D&C 42:42). The Lord has said that unless the idler changes his ways, he will not receive the blessings that those who work will receive. He may not even keep his place in the Church (see D&C 75:29). Of course, it does not matter what work we do as long as it is honest and satisfying work.

With his wife, a husband should organize a family budget. The income he acquires is not his alone—it belongs to the entire family. He is responsible to see that the financial needs of every family member are being met, not just his own. When he puts forth his best efforts to provide for the physical needs of his family, the Lord will bless him, and his wife and children can carry out their proper tasks in the family.

- Show visual 12-a, "Families who work together are blessed both temporally and spiritually."

Children should be encouraged and allowed to receive as much education as possible to make sure they are prepared for their life's work. As far as possible, they should not be taken from school in order to work. This does not mean our children should not have work to do in the home. President Harold B. Lee instructed parents to give special chores to children to keep them from boredom and allow them to develop mature work habits (see "Preparing Our Youth," *Ensign,* Mar. 1971, 3).

One duty children could be given is to care for a family garden. We have been counseled to plant family gardens to produce some of our own food needs and then to store as much food as possible. President Spencer W. Kimball counseled each family to "grow all the food that you feasibly can on your own property. . . . Develop your skills in your home preservation and storage. We reaffirm the previous counsel the Church has always given, to acquire and maintain a year's supply" (in Conference Report, Apr. 1976, 170–71; or *Ensign,* May 1976, 124).

- What are some tasks we can do as a family to teach our children to work? When we are unable to provide for the physical needs of our families, where can we obtain help? (We should always seek help first from family members and relatives who may be in a position to help. If they can't help us, we should turn to the Church and contact our quorum leaders. Government welfare agencies should be contacted only if the Church is unable to help us in the ways we need help.)

*Providing for the Spiritual Needs of the Family*

To meet the spiritual needs of our family we can:

1. Teach the gospel to our wife and children.

2. Have daily family prayer.

3. Make our home a place that invites the Spirit of the Lord to abide with us.

4. Pay tithes and offerings to the Lord.

5. Hold worthwhile family home evenings.

These are all sacred responsibilities. The Doctrine and Covenants points out the importance of one of these duties in particular.

- Have class members read Doctrine and Covenants 68:25, 28. What has the Lord commanded us to teach our children?

A father must make sure that his family is taught the gospel in the home. One of the best ways to begin this teaching is in family home evening. This provides a regular time for us to talk with and instruct our families. The First Presidency has urged all parents "to meet regularly with their families on Monday evenings, there to teach them the scriptures . . . and to bear testimony to them. Parents should take these opportunities to get close to their children, to listen to their problems and [goals], and to give them the personal direction that they need so much" ("Message from the First Presidency," *Family Home Evening* manual, 1976–77, 3).

For a father to properly teach his children, he must organize his time to be home with his family often. He also needs to show the joy of living the gospel in his own life by faithfully paying tithes and offerings to the Church, accepting and fulfilling Church callings, and keeping the other commandments.

- How can the Church help us teach our children?

**Blessings to Fathers and Families**

- Show visual 12-b, "King Benjamin provided for both the physical and the spiritual needs of his family."

The Book of Mormon teaches us about a great prophet-king and father, King Benjamin (see Mosiah 2:12, 14). Even though he was a king and a prophet, he worked with his own hands to provide for his family. He did not expect others to support him. As fathers, we should follow his example and provide for our families.

*12-a, Families who work together are blessed both temporally and spiritually.*

Abraham is another father we can pattern our lives after. Because of his faithfulness, he was promised a righteous family and a great posterity (see Genesis 17:3–8). Abraham was blessed for his diligence in following the Lord and properly providing for his family. We can have these same blessings as we take care of the spiritual and temporal needs of our families. In addition, love will increase in our homes, and our families will progress spiritually.

**Conclusion**

The following story tells how blessings came to a father and his family as he accepted and lived the gospel:

Before Joseph Garcia joined the Church, he enjoyed drinking with his friends and spent little time at home. As a result, his wife often had to take small cleaning jobs to earn money to help support the family. His children barely knew him. They feared him more than they respected or loved him.

One day, however, he was introduced to some missionaries of The Church of Jesus Christ of Latter-day Saints. After six months of meetings with the missionaries, his life completely changed. He quit keeping company with his friends in the bars and soon joined the Church. He began spending time with his children, holding family home evenings and enjoying outings with them and his wife. He planned a careful family budget which allowed his wife to quit working and spend all of her time at home.

He quickly found that he enjoyed his home and the time he spent with his wife more than he ever enjoyed his former friends. His children learned to love him and today are trying to follow his example of righteous living.

**Challenges**

Evaluate how well you are doing in meeting the spiritual and physical needs of your family.

Commit yourself to fulfilling the needs of your family.

Work out a plan with your wife and children to bring your lives in line with the scriptures and the counsel of Church leaders.

**Additional Scriptures**

- 1 Timothy 5:8 (fathers must provide for their families)

- Mosiah 27:14, 22–24 (the Lord hears the prayers of fathers for their children)

*12-b, King Benjamin provided for both the physical and the
spiritual needs of his family.*

- Doctrine and Covenants 68:30–31 (the children of idlers grow up in wickedness)

- Doctrine and Covenants 75:28–29 (fathers to provide for family members)

**Teacher Preparation**

Before presenting this lesson:

1. Read *Gospel Principles* chapters 27, "Work and Personal Responsibility," and 36, "The Family Can Be Eternal."

2. Assign class members to present any stories, scriptures, or quotations you wish.

# COUNSELING WITH FAMILY MEMBERS

*Lesson 13*

---

The purpose of this lesson is to help us strengthen our families by counseling with our wives and children.

**Introduction**

- Have class members sing "Love at Home" (*Hymns*, no. 294; or *Gospel Principles*, 352).

**Fathers Should Lead, Guide, and Direct in Righteousness**

Our earthly homes are the beginning of heavenly homes. The fathers who know this realize that they have a sacred duty to lead, guide, and direct their families in righteousness. President N. Eldon Tanner said: "Every Latter-day Saint home should be a model home, where the father is the head of the household, but presiding with love, and in complete harmony with the righteous desires of the mother. Together they should be seeking the same goals for the family, and the children should feel the love and harmony that exists" ("Fatherhood," *Ensign*, June 1977, 2).

As married priesthood bearers, we have the responsibility of raising a righteous family, but of course we do not do this alone. We have the help of our wives. Together we can build a strong marriage and bring our family back to the presence of the Lord. This means we need to love and counsel with our wives if we are to enjoy the Lord's Spirit in our homes.

**Showing Love and Consideration for Our Wives**

- Read Ephesians 5:25 and Mosiah 4:14.

The Lord instructs us in these scriptures to establish homes of peace and love. To have such homes, we need to make sure a pattern of sincere loving and sharing is established when our marriage begins. If such a pattern is not now in our homes, we should seek to develop it. This requires praying together regularly, showing love and respect for each other, and studying the scriptures together. Perhaps most importantly, it means keeping the commandments of God and the covenants made at the time of our marriage vows.

A strong priesthood leader is kind to and thoughtful of his wife (see Ephesians 5:25). President J. Reuben Clark Jr. stated that if a family is to become a celestial family, the husband and wife must love, honor, and respect each other. They must be patient with each other and be loyal to their marriage vows. Their faith should "cover the home as a kindly light." If they do these things, their obedience to God will "guide and cheer them" (see *Immortality and Eternal Life, vol. 2* [Melchizedek Priesthood study guide, 1969], 14–15).

- What are some things we can do to show love and consideration for our wives? How can showing love and consideration for our wives help us establish homes of peace and love?

### Counseling with Our Wives

- Show visual 13-a, "Family leadership is much easier and more effective when a husband counsels with his wife."

It is important that we communicate with our wives. Most marriage and family problems can be overcome if we counsel with our wives—and seek the help and guidance of the Lord.

- Read Alma 37:37. How can counseling with the Lord help us?

If we are to be wise priesthood holders, we must prayerfully discuss problems and goals with our wives and include our wives when we make decisions. If we love our wives, we will always seek their ideas and assistance rather than try to solve major family problems on our own. To do this, we should set aside a specific time when we can discuss children, finances, the gospel, family home evenings, and any other individual and family concerns we each have. Only in this way will we be unified in guiding our families.

Both husbands and wives are important in the marriage partnership. Some men feel that because they have the priesthood, they are in a position to make all the decisions, but the scriptures tell us this is wrong.

- Read Doctrine and Covenants 121:39, 41.

It is a misuse of the priesthood to "exercise unrighteous dominion." As priesthood holders, we have a duty to listen to our wives in love and concern. And when we listen, we should not listen as their superiors, for they are partners with us and our equals. The following experience shows how one priesthood holder counseled with his wife.

Brother and Sister Jackson were both wise and well educated. Each could have made many family decisions alone. But instead, they always sat down and discussed problems and possible solutions together. At least once a week, usually on Sunday evening, they sat at the kitchen table and talked over family problems. Sometimes the

*13-a, Family leadership is much easier and more effective
when a husband counsels with his wife.*

children were brought into the discussion. By counseling together, this couple nearly always agreed on how their children should be raised. They sometimes expressed differing opinions, but they were always respectful and loving to each other. They were wise in always asking for each other's valuable advice, and they set a pattern of a near-celestial home that all of their six children now try to follow in their own homes.

- How can counseling together help a husband and wife avoid arguments and problems in their home? How can it increase love in their marriage?

### Counseling with Our Families

- Show visual 13-b, "Holding family councils helps a father lead his children in righteousness."

After a husband and wife have counseled together, they should call their children together and discuss with them their family goals and plans. Holding council with the entire family is valuable. It can improve family life and deepen the love between family members. Children who are made aware of family plans in advance will know what the others are doing, and order and harmony will result. When possible, children should be allowed to share in decision making and should help carry out these decisions.

- When is a good time to hold family council? (Family home evening is an ideal time, but family council should not replace the lesson.) What are some areas that could be discussed in such a council?

- Show visual 13-c, "Fathers can strengthen their relationships with their children by counseling with them."

It is also important that fathers counsel privately with each of their children. "Only good results occur when a father interviews his sons and daughters regularly. He can know their problems and their hopes. He can align himself with them as their unconditional friend" (A. Theodore Tuttle, in Conference Report, Oct. 1973, 87; or *Ensign*, Jan. 1974, 67).

- What are some things you could discuss with your children in such interviews? How could this bring you closer to them? (Encourage the brethren to use interviews to *listen* to the concerns of their children.)

Counseling with our children does not always need to be a formal situation. We should take every opportunity, whenever and wherever it comes, to listen to their problems. In counseling with them, we should look at their problems from their point of view. We should not laugh at their concerns or think that their problems are unimportant, but should lovingly listen to them and try to understand and help them.

*13-b, Holding family councils helps a father lead his children in righteousness.*

"It is wonderful when a father or a mother will sit down with a son or a daughter and discuss a personal problem (and they have their problems, which, if we are wise, we will not minimize). There are pressures, and enticements, and even unjust accusations against which our sons and daughters need to be fortified. . . . In such heart-to-heart talks, parents will help to set objectives for their children" (ElRay L. Christiansen, in Conference Report, Apr. 1972, 43; or *Ensign*, July 1972, 55).

- What things should a young man discuss with his parents? What things should a father discuss with his children? (You may want to remind class members that everyone has different challenges.)

Elder Richard L. Evans, in talking to children about counseling with their parents, said: "You and they together have the privilege, the right, the duty, to sit down and share your thoughts and consider your decisions with one another, that both of you together may be listened to and respected—and work and pray and plan together for the wholeness of your happiness—always and forever" ("As Parents and Children Come to Common Ground," *Improvement Era*, May 1956, 342).

**Conclusion**

We are promised that if we are faithful we will live in harmony and peace in the celestial kingdom. But we must begin now to achieve unity and love, for it does not just happen. President David O. McKay said: "I can imagine few, if any, things more objectionable in the home than the absence of unity and harmony. On the other hand, I know that a home in which unity, mutual helpfulness, and love abide is just a bit of heaven on earth" (in Conference Report, Oct. 1967, 7; or *Improvement Era*, Dec. 1967, 34).

As we counsel with our wives and children, we will strengthen both them and ourselves and increase the love and unity in our families.

**Challenges**

Pray and counsel regularly with your wife.

Hold a family council.

Establish a time to interview each of your children, remembering to be prayerful and considerate in talking with them.

**Additional Scriptures**

- Galatians 5:22 (the fruit of the Spirit)

- Jacob 2:35 (the effect of a bad example on family members)

- Jacob 3:7 (the importance of love between husband and wife)

*13-c, Fathers can strengthen their relationships with their children by counseling with them.*

- Doctrine and Covenants 121:36–38 (the priesthood should be used only in righteousness)

**Teacher Preparation**

Before presenting this lesson:

1. Read *Gospel Principles* chapter 37, "Family Responsibilities."

2. Assign class members to present any stories, scriptures, or quotations you wish.

# LEADING FAMILY PRAYER

*Lesson   1 4*

The purpose of this lesson is to encourage us to have daily family prayer.

### Introduction

- Show visual 14-a, "We should pray as families each morning and night."

As fathers, we should call our families together for family prayer to give thanks to our Heavenly Father and ask for His guidance. Elder Spencer W. Kimball said:

"I have interviewed numerous heads of families . . . who have admitted that their family prayers were irregular, and more frequently missed than held. Some say they try to have family prayer once a day, and others shrug it off by saying they cannot get their families together. This casual attitude toward the vital matter of prayer disturbs me greatly. . . .

". . . The Church urges that there be family prayer every night and every morning. It is a kneeling prayer. . . . All members of the family, including the little ones, should have opportunity to [say] the prayer" ("I Kneeled Down before My Maker," *Instructor,* Apr. 1966, 132).

### Family Prayer: A Help in Resisting Temptation

We have been commanded to pray to our Heavenly Father, especially with our families.

- Read 3 Nephi 18:18–21. What important purpose does the Savior give for prayer? In what ways does prayer help us to resist temptation?

Regular family prayer can help our families resist the temptations of Satan. Through prayer, we can draw closer to our Heavenly Father, and we can receive strength and be better able to overcome our problems.

### Teaching Prayer through Example

As fathers we should call our families to prayer and set the example. In the Doctrine and Covenants, fathers and mothers are commanded to

*14-a, We should pray as families each morning and night.*

teach their children to pray (see D&C 68:28). The best way to teach the principle of prayer to children is by example. If we make the effort to pray with them, our children will learn the importance of prayer and practice it in their lives.

Leading and teaching our children are duties that all fathers have; one does not need to hold the Melchizedek Priesthood to lead his family in prayer.

### Making Family Prayer Work in Your Home

In order to make family prayer work in our homes, we should set special times for prayer in the home. Our Church leaders have told us to gather the family together twice a day. To do this, we will need to find the most convenient times for our family to get together. It should be a regular time when all family members will be at home. These times may come in the morning before we leave the house for work and school and shortly before the children go to bed in the evening. Elder Spencer W. Kimball taught: "Many have found the most effective time is at the breakfast and at the dinner table. Then it is least difficult to get the family members together" ("I Kneeled Down before My Maker," *Instructor*, Apr. 1966, 132).

- Invite class members to describe what they have done to establish a regular pattern of prayer in their homes.

Morning prayers should include our plans for the day. Evening prayers should thank the Lord for His protection and guidance. The blessing on the food at each meal should not take the place of the regular family prayer, but can be included in it if we hold family prayer just before eating.

Some other blessings we should pray for are mentioned by Amulek in the Book of Mormon.

- Read Alma 34:23–25.

Our own lists of things to pray for might be different from Amulek's list, but the principles he spoke of are the same. One principle is that we should pray about our everyday activities. Another is that we should pray for strength to resist the temptations of the devil. Each family should look at its goals and needs and pray sincerely for the things most necessary to them. If we do this, our prayers will be sincere and effective, not just words we repeat day after day. As fathers, we should help our little children avoid repeating the same words every time they pray. In doing this, we must seek the influence of the Spirit (see D&C 42:14). Whatever we do to teach our children to pray, we must never force or embarrass them.

We must not become discouraged if we have problems holding effective family prayers. Often, Satan is behind the problem.

- Read 2 Nephi 32:8. Why do you think Satan tries to stop us from praying?

Satan will try to stop family prayers because he can more easily influence a family that does not pray regularly. The habit of holding family prayer, therefore, should be so strong that even when fathers are not home, their wives will call the family together. If both we and our wives are going to be away, we should assign an older child to lead the family in prayer.

- How can youth support and encourage family prayer?

**Spiritual Blessings through Family Prayer**

Great blessings will come to us as we hold family prayer. Love and understanding will increase, and Satan's influence in the home will be diminished. A feeling of peace will fill our hearts as we realize that we are properly fulfilling a commandment.

Family prayer is one step in creating an eternal home. President Spencer W. Kimball said that "when we kneel in family prayer, our children . . . are learning habits that will stay with them all through their lives. If we do not take time for prayers, what we are actually saying to our children is, 'Well, it isn't very important, anyway. . . .' On the other hand, what a joyous thing it is to establish such customs and habits in the home that when parents visit their children . . . after they are married they just naturally kneel with them in the usual, established manner of prayer!" (*The Miracle of Forgiveness* [1969], 253).

**Conclusion**

We may wonder at times if our children are really learning about Christ and feeling His presence in family prayer. But children are sometimes closer to the Spirit than we realize. President Heber J. Grant wrote about the following experience he had with prayer as a child in the home of President Brigham Young:

"I knelt down . . . in [Brigham Young's] home . . . at family prayers, as a child and as a young man. I bear witness that as a little child, upon more than one occasion, because of the inspiration of the Lord to Brigham Young while he was [asking] God for guidance, I have lifted my head, turned and looked at the place where Brigham Young was praying, to see if the Lord was . . . there. It seemed to me that he talked to the Lord as one man would talk to another" (*Gospel Standards*, comp. G. Homer Durham [1941], 223–24).

Prayer should be as inspiring an experience for our children as it was for Heber J. Grant. The following story shows what can happen when family prayer is used the way it should be:

"One father, a quiet, unassuming man, found it hard to express his love for his family. At his wife's prompting they began holding family prayer, and it became an opportunity to voice what was in his heart. To their daughter, who had misinterpreted her father's manner as indifference, the experience was a revelation. His prayers were simple and sometimes clumsily worded, but to hear him say 'Bless my lovely daughter to do good' thrilled her.

"A timid boy who thought of himself only as a 'scaredy cat' felt new pride and self-esteem when his father and mother thanked God for their 'kind, gentle son.' And the boy's self-confidence continued to grow through prayer when even his little brother thanked Heavenly Father for his 'big, strong brother.'

"In preparation for a family outing in our own family, my husband asked the Lord to bless our family to get along and to enjoy each other's company. The preaching we had done had gone unheard, but that reverent prayer brought cooperation.

"Our teenage son was tense and sullen whenever we tried to discuss any problem with him. We decided it was important to plan the discussion when he would be most receptive, and that seemed to be at family prayer time in the mornings. It was then that the house was quiet and we shared a humble, sincere feeling. We found the tenseness eased when prayer preceded our discussions.

"During these quiet moments of family prayer, we are keeping in touch with each other and with our Father in heaven" (Ann H. Banks, "The Extra Blessings of Prayer," *Ensign*, Jan. 1976, 37).

- Invite class members to share successful experiences they have had with family prayer. Consider ending the lesson with "God, Our Father, Hear Us Pray" (*Hymns*, no. 170; or *Gospel Principles*, 329) or "Prayer Is the Soul's Sincere Desire" (*Hymns*, no. 145).

### Challenges

Hold family prayers if you are not holding them now.

Evaluate your prayers if you are already having them regularly.

Discuss with your wife and children how to improve your family prayers.

### Additional Scriptures

- Matthew 5:44 (we should pray for those who persecute us)

- Matthew 7:7 (answers are given to sincere prayers)

- Matthew 26:41 (we should pray for protection against temptation)

- Alma 13:28 (we should pray for protection against temptation)

- Alma 37:36–37 (we should pray about all our activities)

- Doctrine and Covenants 88:119 (we should establish a house of prayer)

- Doctrine and Covenants 88:126 (we should pray always)

**Teacher Preparation**

Before presenting this lesson:

1. Read *Gospel Principles* chapter 8, "Praying to Our Heavenly Father."

2. If you desire, assign a class member to tell a successful experience he has had with family prayer.

3. Assign class members to present any stories, scriptures, or quotations you wish.

# THE HOME: A CENTER FOR GOSPEL STUDY

*Lesson 15*

The purpose of this lesson is to encourage us to make the home a center for gospel learning.

## Introduction

Enos was the son of a prophet and often heard his father talk of eternal truths. One day Enos went into the forest to hunt. He recorded the experience as follows:

"The words which I had often heard my father speak concerning eternal life . . . sunk deep into my heart.

"And my soul hungered; and I kneeled down before my Maker" (Enos 1:3–4).

After praying all day long, he heard a voice telling him that his sins were forgiven. The experience was so important to Enos that he taught the gospel and rejoiced in it the rest of his life.

Enos is an example of a young man who was properly taught the gospel in his home. An Old Testament writer wrote: "Train up a child in the way he should go: and when he is old, he will not depart from it" (Proverbs 22:6). If we follow this counsel as fathers, we too may be blessed with loyal children who obey us and the Lord.

## Making Our Homes Centers for Learning

The family is the most important organization both in the Church and in society. Indeed, it is the only organization that will exist eternally. For this reason the Lord has commanded us to make our homes places where families can learn the gospel and progress together.

- Read Doctrine and Covenants 68:25–28. Where do our children gain basic knowledge about the world we live in? Where can they learn about eternal life?

Children learn about this life in the home, at school, and from their play-mates. But neither the public schools nor their friends can teach our children about the gospel. This sacred responsibility is ours, given to us by Heavenly Father. If we fail to teach our children what He would have us teach them in this life, we are in danger of losing them in eternity.

Of course, before we can teach the gospel to our children, we must first learn it ourselves. Elder Marion G. Romney said: "Let every priesthood bearer, in the majesty and power of his calling, set in order his own house; let him regularly observe home evening and otherwise bring up his 'children in light and truth' (D&C 93:40)" (in Conference Report, Apr. 1969, 110; or *Improvement Era,* June 1969, 97).

This means that, with our wives, we are responsible for teaching gospel principles to our children. To fulfill that responsibility, we must begin the practice of gospel study in our homes with our wives and encourage our children to follow our example. King Benjamin told parents:

"Ye will not suffer your children . . . that they transgress the laws of God, and fight and quarrel one with another, and serve the devil. . . .

"But ye will teach them to walk in the ways of truth and soberness; ye will teach them to love one another, and to serve one another" (Mosiah 4:14–15).

**Our Family Plan for Gospel Learning**

If we are to follow the counsel of the prophets, we need to plan with our wives how best to teach our children. Although each of us may accomplish this purpose in a different way, we must be willing to work out the best plan to make our home a place for gospel learning. (The remainder of this lesson provides suggestions on how to encourage gospel learning in our families.)

*Create an Atmosphere for Learning*

Our homes should be a place where our children feel free to talk with us. A home that is filled with tension does not encourage children to ask questions and express their feelings. President David O. McKay taught parents: "Show a willingness to answer questions. A child that is asking questions is contributing happiness to your life" (*Gospel Ideals* [1953], 480). We should encourage children to ask questions, especially about gospel subjects. We may not always know the answers to their questions, but we can always search them out together.

▪ In what specific ways can we encourage gospel discussions in our homes?

*Pray with the Family*

One way we can teach our children is through family prayer. When we pray, we can communicate our hopes, concerns, and ideals for our family. We can teach concern for the needs of others as we pray for family members and others. And we can teach appreciation for blessings as we express our gratitude to our Heavenly Father.

### Have Gospel Discussions at Meals and Bedtime

Other times to encourage gospel discussions are at meals and at bedtime. In such settings, children can be encouraged to ask questions, and adults can explain gospel principles. To encourage children's questions, we can share gospel stories from the Book of Mormon or the Bible or from our own spiritual experiences.

### Study the Scriptures Regularly

- Show visual 15-a, "The home should be a center of gospel study."

To promote regular scripture study, a shelf or book stand could be set aside as a gospel library. Here, books, pictures, tapes, a tape player, and other teaching aids could be kept for the whole family to use. The standard works of the Church and the *Gospel Principles* manual should be included in our library. If possible, each child should have his or her own copy of the Book of Mormon and the Bible.

We can study the scriptures individually and as families. To encourage individual study, parents must set the example. The following are ways we can study the scriptures individually:

1. Read the scriptures from beginning to end, reading one or more chapters each day, or for a certain amount of time each day.

2. Study the scriptures by topic (such as *prayer* or *obedience*), locating all the references about that topic.

3. Search the scriptures to find the answer to a specific problem we have.

4. Make a list of scriptures that inspire us.

5. Cross-reference scriptures in a regular study plan.

- Discuss with class members other ways to study the scriptures.

To study the gospel as families, each father must schedule a time with his wife and children when they can get together specifically for this purpose. The following are ways we can study the scriptures as families:

1. Plan for a certain amount of time for scripture study each morning before we leave for work and the children leave for school, or hold a short family scripture study in the evening before the children go to bed.

2. Tell stories from the scriptures to the younger children.

3. Select special scripture verses, write them on a card, and post the card on a bulletin board or wall for all the family to see.

*15-a, The home should be a center of gospel study.*

4. Encourage family members to memorize scriptures.

5. Choose a scripture that teaches a principle and decide on a way to practice the principle taught. For example, read together Matthew 25:31–40, and then help a needy family. Or read James 1:26–27 and Galatians 6:2; then help an elderly person.

Whatever approach we choose to follow, we should always begin our scripture study with prayer, asking Heavenly Father for guidance and help in understanding. After our study period, we should think about what we have read and how to apply the gospel principles we have read in our lives.

Bishop H. Burke Peterson of the Presiding Bishopric said: "There shouldn't be—there mustn't be—one family in this Church that doesn't take the time to read from the scriptures every day. Every family can do it in their own way" (in Conference Report, Apr. 1975, 79; or *Ensign*, May 1975, 53–54).

▪ Have the previously assigned class member who has achieved success in studying the scriptures with his family report on his method. Or have a previously assigned Aaronic Priesthood youth tell why he feels he should learn the gospel in his youth, especially before going on a mission. (He may want to read Alma 37:35.)

### Hold Family Home Evening Regularly

▪ Show visual 15-b, "Family home evening is a good time to study the gospel as a family."

Family home evening is a good time to teach our children the gospel. Those of us who have the family home evening manual should use it. If no manual is available, we should study the scriptures and the *Gospel Principles* manual, listen to gospel recordings, or share our feelings about the Church. Creating a pleasant, happy atmosphere will help the children enjoy the evening and help them participate more willingly.

### Bear Our Testimonies to Our Children

When the opportunity presents itself, we should bear our testimonies to our children. The opportunity to bear our testimonies may come at mealtime, during scripture study, during family home evening, or in gospel discussions with our children. When our children hear us bear our testimonies and see us live the commandments, their understanding of the gospel will increase.

▪ Ask class members to share experiences they have had teaching the gospel to their children.

*15-b, Family home evening is a good time to study the gospel as a family.*

## Conclusion

As we study the gospel individually and with our families, our testimonies and our homes will be strengthened. Because we are trying to live closer to Jesus Christ and Heavenly Father, we will find answers to our problems and have a greater peace of mind. Elder Bruce R. McConkie said: "We want to have peace and joy and happiness in this life and be inheritors of eternal life in the world to come. These are the two greatest blessings that it is possible for people to inherit. We can gain them by reading and learning the words of eternal life, here and now, and by keeping the commandments" ("Drink from the Fountain," *Ensign,* Apr. 1975, 70).

## Challenges

Study the gospel regularly.

Hold family prayer daily.

Take every opportunity to teach the gospel to your family.

## Additional Scriptures

- Romans 15:4 (all scripture was written to help us)

- 2 Timothy 3:14–17 (the need for scripture)

- 2 Nephi 4:15 (we should ponder the scriptures and teach them to our children)

- Doctrine and Covenants 1:37 (we should search the scriptures)

---

## Teacher Preparation

Before presenting this lesson:

1. Read the additional scriptures listed at the end of this lesson.

2. If you desire, assign class members to share successful experiences they have had in studying the scriptures as a family or teaching the gospel to their children. You may also want to assign an Aaronic Priesthood youth to tell why he feels it is important to learn the gospel in his youth.

3. Assign class members to present any stories, scriptures, or quotations you wish.

# TEACHING THE GOSPEL

*Lesson   1 6*

The purpose of this lesson is to help us recognize our responsibility to teach the gospel effectively.

## Introduction

In a revelation given through the Prophet Joseph Smith, the Lord has commanded us to teach:

"And I give unto you a commandment that you shall teach one another the doctrine of the kingdom.

"Teach ye diligently and my grace shall attend you, that you may be instructed more perfectly in theory, in principle, in doctrine, in the law of the gospel, in all things that pertain unto the kingdom of God, that are expedient for you to understand" (D&C 88:77–78).

The possibilities for teaching the gospel are many and varied. We can teach our families, our friends, our neighbors, our coworkers, and our school classmates. We can teach members of the Church in organized classes, and nonmembers of the Church as we associate with them at work or in our neighborhoods.

## Preparing to Teach the Gospel

- Show visual 16-a, "Lessons should be prepared with each class member in mind," and 16-b, "Lesson preparation includes scripture study and prayer."

If we are to become good teachers, we must prepare well. "No teacher can teach that which he does not know," President David O. McKay told us. "No teacher can teach that which he does not see and feel" (*Treasures of Life* [1962], 476).

### Preparing Ourselves Spiritually

If we prepare ourselves spiritually, the Holy Ghost will guide and help us as we teach. The following are suggestions for how to prepare spiritually to teach:

*16-a, Lessons should be prepared with each class member in mind.*

*Pray.* We should pray often to ask the Lord to guide us as we study and prepare. We should also pray for the individuals we teach.

*Study the scriptures.* As we study the scriptures, we learn about the Lord and increase our knowledge of the truth.

*Live the gospel.* When we live the teachings of the gospel, we receive strength, peace, and happiness that will be an example to those we teach.

*Be humble.* Humility helps us avoid seeking honor for ourselves or relying too much on our own strength. The Lord taught, "Be thou humble; and the Lord thy God shall lead thee by the hand, and give thee answer to thy prayers" (D&C 112:10).

### Preparing a Lesson

President David O. McKay was a professional teacher before he was called to be a General Authority of the Church. He suggested four steps in preparing a lesson for a class:

*Determine the objective.* The objective is the idea you want the class members to learn and put into action. Write your goal and think about it as you prepare the lesson.

*Know the lesson material.* Know the lesson well enough so that you can teach it in your own words. Of course, scriptures and quotations may be read from the manual.

*Gather visual aids.* To create interest in the lesson, use interesting visual aids, such as objects, charts, pictures, or other helpful items. Creating interest in a lesson is important in teaching people of all ages.

*Organize the lesson materials.* Have everything ready that you will need during your lesson, such as chalk, eraser, paper, pencils, and visual aids. These should be arranged in the order in which they will be used in the lesson to help you avoid confusion while giving the lesson.

### Learning to Love Those We Teach

Another important part of effective gospel teaching is to love those we teach. Elder Boyd K. Packer said: "The good teacher has already studied the lesson. The superb teacher also studies the students—studies them seriously and intently. . . . As you study carefully the features and expressions of your students, there may well within your heart a warmth of Christian compassion. . . . Compassion is a feeling akin to inspiration; it is love that will compel you to find the way to do the work of the Lord—feeding His sheep" ("Study Your Students," *Instructor,* Jan. 1963, 17).

Students who are loved will become more self-confident and will desire to improve themselves. They will be more attentive, cooperative, and helpful in class. Most of all, students who are loved will learn how to love others.

### Teaching with the Spirit

If a teacher is to love his students, he must be sensitive to inspiration from the Lord. Only in this way will he truly understand the needs of his students. President Brigham Young said, "After all our endeavors to obtain wisdom from the best books, etc., there still remains an open fountain for all: 'If any man lack wisdom let him ask of God' " (*Discourses of Brigham Young* [1954], 261).

The ability to teach is a gift we receive from our Father in Heaven. If we ask Him, He will inspire us as we prepare the lesson, as we seek to know and love the students, and as we teach. And when we teach with His Spirit, we teach with power. (For further information, see lesson 18, "Teaching by the Power of the Holy Ghost.")

### Teaching in the Home

- Show visual 16-c, "A father is responsible for teaching his children the gospel."

From the creation of the earth, we have been told by the Lord that we have a great responsibility to teach our children the gospel. A good time to teach our families is on Sunday or during family home evening on Monday, but there are many other appropriate times. The following story illustrates how one father learned to teach his family:

Several fathers were involved in a study concerning family home evening. Most of them expressed feelings such as, "I'm not a teacher; I never was and I never will be." They were promised that if they would call the family together each week in a warm and relaxed atmosphere, the teaching part would not be the problem that they imagined it to be.

One father, whose name was Jerry, didn't seem enthusiastic about the request. He attempted to get out of the request by saying, "I can't teach." But he had committed himself, and he was held to his commitment.

Three months later, when approached about his experience, he was very friendly and warm, and his children expressed enthusiasm for what had happened in the family home evenings.

His wife said, "It has been a wonderful experience for us. The very best lessons we have had were those Jerry taught."

Jerry looked down for a time and remained silent. Then he remarked, "Aw, I didn't do so good."

His wife was very sincere as she replied, "Jerry, when you taught us it just seemed so powerful. It just seemed as if we were a family. We'll never forget the things you said."

Jerry was deeply touched by these heartfelt words. He looked up and said, "I guess I did do pretty good. I didn't want to have these family home evenings. I just didn't feel I could do it. But one night after my wife had taught a lesson one week and my daughter another week, I decided I'd try one."

His eyes grew moist as he said: "I'll never forget the feeling I had in my heart as I talked about good things with my family. It just seemed that for the first time I was the father that I was supposed to be" (see George D. Durrant, *Love at Home: Starring Father* [1976], 41–43).

This story illustrates what can happen when we assume our responsibility to teach our families.

- Ask several brethren to share their experiences in teaching the gospel to their children.

Elder Boyd K. Packer said: "Much of what we do is teaching. Showing a youngster how to tie his shoe, . . . helping a daughter with a new recipe, giving a talk in church, bearing testimony, conducting a leadership meeting, and, of course, teaching a class—all of this is teaching, and we are doing it constantly. . . . We are teaching when we preach or speak or respond in meetings" (*Teach Ye Diligently* [1975], 2–3).

**Teaching in the Church**

Much of the teaching we do is done informally as we talk with one another. But the Church also provides us with many opportunities to teach in organized classes.

Elder Boyd K. Packer wrote: "Every member of the Church teaches for virtually his whole lifetime. . . . We have teachers serving in all the organizations of the Church. A great deal of teaching is done in the priesthood quorums; indeed, all priesthood holders are eligible for appointment as priesthood home *teachers*. . . . The Church moves forward sustained by the power of the teaching that is accomplished. The work of the Kingdom is impeded if teaching is not efficiently done" (*Teach Ye Diligently* [1975], 2–3).

*16-b, Lesson preparation includes scripture study and prayer.*

Sometimes our teaching is not done in a classroom, but through our associations with others in the Church. The following stories are examples of teaching done outside the classroom:

"Bishop Fred Carroll entered the scene when our family moved into his ward while I was an over-age deacon in the Aaronic Priesthood. This great man probably spoke no more than fifty words to me directly, yet twenty-five of them remain indelibly imprinted on my mind. I am certain that this good bishop was never aware of the tremendous impact he had on me with those twenty-five golden words, given to me one day quietly and privately: 'I have been noticing how reverent you are in our church meetings. It is a fine example you set for the other boys to follow.'

"Just a few words, but oh, how powerful! To me they had more effect than hundreds of assignments have had since. Up to that time I never did see myself as being particularly reverent. I am quite sure that Bishop Carroll mistook my shy, reserved manner for reverence. Yet that did not matter. From that time on I started wondering about the meaning of reverence in my life. I soon began to feel reverent. After all, if Bishop Carroll thought I was reverent perhaps I really was! The attitude which developed in me because Bishop Carroll planted a seed has since grown to be a guiding influence in my life" (Lynn F. Stoddard, "The Magic Touch," *Instructor*, Sept. 1970, 326–27).

Elder Thomas S. Monson wrote:

"When dedicated teachers respond to [the Savior's] gentle invitation, 'Come learn of me,' they learn, but they also become partakers of his divine power. It was my experience as a small boy to come under the influence of such a teacher. In our Sunday School class, she taught us concerning the creation of the world, the fall of Adam, the atoning sacrifice of Jesus. She brought to her classroom as honored guests Moses, Joshua, Peter, Thomas, Paul, and Jesus the Christ. Though we did not see them, we learned to love, honor, and emulate them.

"Never was her teaching so dynamic nor its impact more everlasting as one Sunday morning when she sadly announced to us the passing of a classmate's mother. We had missed Billy that morning, but knew not the reason for his absence. The lesson featured the theme, 'It is more blessed to give than to receive.' Midway through the lesson, our teacher closed the manual and opened our eyes and our ears and our hearts to the glory of God. She asked, 'How much money do we have in our class party fund?'

"Depression days prompted a proud answer: 'Four dollars and seventy-five cents.'

*16-c, A father is responsible for teaching his children the gospel.*

"Then ever so gently she suggested: 'Billy's family is hard-pressed and grief-stricken. What would you think of the possibility of visiting the family members this morning and giving to them your fund?'

"Ever shall I remember the tiny band walking those three city blocks, entering Billy's home, greeting him, his brother, sisters, and father. Noticeably absent was his mother. Always I shall treasure the tears which glistened in the eyes of all as the white envelope containing our precious party fund passed from the delicate hand of our teacher to the needy hand of a heartbroken father. We fairly skipped our way back to the chapel. Our hearts were lighter than they had ever been; our joy more full; our understanding more profound. A God-inspired teacher had taught her boys and girls an eternal lesson of divine truth. 'It is more blessed to give than to receive' " (in Conference Report, Apr. 1970, 99; or *Improvement Era*, June 1970, 91).

### Teaching in the World

Every member of the Church is a missionary with the responsibility for teaching the gospel by word or deed to every person with whom he comes in contact. We made a covenant at the time of baptism "to stand as witnesses of God at all times and in all things, and in all places that we may be in, even until death" (Mosiah 18:9). As we teach our friends and neighbors, we should do so in mildness and meekness (see D&C 38:40–41).

We have been given a great responsibility, not just to teach our children or members of the Church, but to teach every person with whom we come in contact.

### Conclusion

"President David O. McKay said, 'There is no greater responsibility in the world than the training of a human soul.' A great part of the personal stewardship of every parent and teacher in the Church is to teach and train" (quoted by Vaughn J. Featherstone, in Conference Report, Oct. 1976, 153; or *Ensign*, Nov. 1976, 103). We have the responsibility to teach the gospel of Jesus Christ to our children, to fellow members of the Church, and to our nonmember neighbors. In order to do this, we must prepare ourselves by studying and living the gospel.

### Challenge

Prepare and teach the lesson for the next family home evening by studying and by praying for the influence of the Holy Ghost.

**Additional Scriptures**

- Deuteronomy 6:1–7 (importance of diligently teaching children)

- Mosiah 4:14–15 (how to teach children properly)

- Doctrine and Covenants 68:25–28 (parents are to teach the gospel to their children)

- Doctrine and Covenants 130:18 (we will keep the intelligence we obtained in this life when we are resurrected)

---

**Teacher Preparation**

Before presenting this lesson:

1. If you desire, assign several class members to share good experiences they have had in teaching their children.

2. Assign class members to present any stories, scriptures, or quotations you wish.

# TEACHING FROM THE SCRIPTURES

*L e s s o n    1 7*

---

The purpose of this lesson is to help us understand why we should teach from the scriptures.

## Introduction

- Display visuals 17-a, "We must study the scriptures if we are to teach from them," and 17-b, "Teaching the gospel requires a good knowledge of the scriptures."

President J. Reuben Clark Jr. once told a group of teachers in the Church: "Your essential . . . duty, is to teach the Gospel of the Lord Jesus Christ. . . . You are to teach this Gospel using as your sources and authorities the Standard Works [scriptures] of the Church, and the words of those whom God has called to lead His people in these last days" (*The Charted Course of the Church in Education* [1938], 9).

The scriptures are the greatest teaching aids available to us. It is important to know them and use them as we teach.

## The Importance of Teaching from the Scriptures

The Lord has clearly taught the importance of knowing the scriptures and teaching with them. During His visit to the Nephites, He said, "Yea, a commandment I give unto you that ye search these things [the scriptures] diligently" (3 Nephi 23:1). We are to search them because they teach us about Jesus Christ and because "they are true and faithful, and the prophecies and promises which are in them shall all be fulfilled" (D&C 1:37; see also 1 Nephi 19:23).

- Read Doctrine and Covenants 68:2–4. What "scriptures" do we have today in addition to the standard works? (The inspired teachings of modern-day Apostles and Prophets.) Where can we find the teachings of modern-day Apostles and Prophets? (Church magazines and general conference reports.) How have you been blessed as you have treated their counsel as scripture?

*17-a, We must study the scriptures if we are to teach from them.*

*17-b, Teaching the gospel requires a good knowledge of the scriptures.*

**Teaching the Scriptures Effectively**

When Lehi and his family arrived at the promised land, Nephi taught his brethren the scriptures in a way that they could understand them: "For I did liken all scriptures unto us," he said, "that it might be for our profit and learning" (1 Nephi 19:23). Likening the scriptures unto ourselves is very important if we are to teach them effectively. Good teachers often compare the scriptures to our own situations by showing how the events of the past apply to the present.

▪ Show visual 17-c, "Nephi and Lehi find the Liahona."

The following story from the Book of Mormon was used in this way by President Spencer W. Kimball:

"Can you think of yourself as being Nephi who heard his father excitedly call attention to something he had found just outside the door of his tent? It was . . . 'a round ball of curious workmanship,' made 'of fine brass,' and none of you had ever seen anything like it before. (1 Ne. 16:10.) . . .

" . . . If you were greatly interested and observed very carefully the workings of this unusual ball, [you would note] that it worked 'according to the faith and diligence and heed' which were given unto it concerning the way you should go (1 Ne. 16:28.) . . . Upon closer examination, you [would note] that there were writings upon the ball that were 'plain to be read' and . . . explained the ways of the Lord. [As you made requests of the Lord, the instructions would change. The change of instructions was according to the faith and diligence of your family. (1 Ne. 16:28)]. . . .

"The ball, or Liahona—which is interpreted to mean a compass—was prepared by the Lord especially to show unto [Lehi] the course which he should travel in the wilderness. Wouldn't you like to have that kind of a ball—each one of you—so that whenever you were in error it would point the right way and write messages to you . . . so that you would always know when you were in error or in the wrong way?

"That, my young brethren, you all have. The Lord gave to every boy, every man, every person, a conscience which tells him everytime he starts to go on the wrong path. He is always told if he is listening; but people can, of course, become so used to hearing the messages that they ignore them until finally they do not register anymore.

"You must realize that you have something like the compass, like the Liahona, in your own system. Every child is given it. . . . If he ignores the Liahona that he has in his own makeup, he eventually may not have it whispering to him. But if we will remember that everyone of us has [a Liahona] that will direct [us] aright, our ship will not get on

*17-c, Nephi and Lehi find the Liahona.*

the wrong course . . . if we listen to the dictates of our own Liahona, which we call the conscience" (in Conference Report, Oct. 1976, 115–17; or *Ensign,* Nov. 1976, 77–79).

- How did President Kimball use the scriptures to teach a truth we can use today?

When we understand the scriptures, we can apply the principles taught in them to situations in our lives. The following examples show how two fathers taught their children from the scriptures.

### *"Judge Not, That Ye Be Not Judged"*

Lara and Todd had been told repeatedly not to leave their bicycles in the driveway. One day their father came home to find both bikes in the driveway. He confronted Todd first. "Todd," he said, "I just found Lara's bike in the driveway. What should I do?"

"You should ground her for a week, like you told us you would," Todd answered.

Later, the father asked Lara: "I just found Todd's bicycle in the driveway. What should I do?"

"Give him another chance; he'll remember next time," Lara responded.

The father then called both children together and had them read Matthew 7:1–2.

- Read Matthew 7:1–2.

When they finished reading these verses, he said: "Todd, you are grounded for one week. Lara, I'll consider this a warning if you'll go out and move the bike right now."

### *"The Laborer Is Worthy of His Hire"*

Ron contracted with his father to wash all the windows in the house for 10 dollars. His brother, Rick, contracted to paint the dining room— also for 10 dollars. It took Ron half a day to do the windows. It took Rick two days to paint the room. When the father paid both boys their $10.00, Rick protested that he should be paid more because he worked longer. In answer, the father read Matthew 20:1–15.

- Read Matthew 20:1–15.

The father concluded by saying that he had kept his part of the bargain, so Rick should go his way and not be angry.

- How can we apply each of the following scriptures to situations in our lives today? Read and discuss in turn Matthew 25:1–13, Enos 1:2–8, and Doctrine and Covenants 40:1–3.

### Preparing to Teach from the Scriptures

President Harold B. Lee stated: "I say that we need to teach our people to find their answers in the scriptures. . . . But the unfortunate thing is that so many of us are not reading the scriptures. We do not know what is in them, and therefore we speculate about the things that we ought to have found in the scriptures themselves. I think that therein is one of our biggest dangers of today" ("Find the Answers in the Scriptures," *Ensign,* Dec. 1972, 3).

No one will force us to study the scriptures. We can always find many excuses for not studying and searching the scriptures. We must commit ourselves to studying the scriptures and work out a regular study plan. If we do, when we are faced with the choice of either reading the scriptures or doing something else, we will choose the scriptures because we have already made the choice.

The ability to read, enjoy, and teach the scriptures not only requires that we plan, but also that we ponder and pray.

- Read Moroni 10:3. What does Moroni tell us about reading the scriptures?

As we read the scriptures, we should ponder them in our hearts. President Marion G. Romney said: "As I have read the scriptures, I have been challenged by the word *ponder.* . . . The dictionary says that *ponder* means 'to weigh mentally, think deeply about, deliberate, meditate.' . . . *Pondering* is, in my feeling, a form of prayer. It has, at least, been an approach to the Spirit of the Lord" (in Conference Report, Apr. 1973, 117; or *Ensign,* July 1973, 90).

Moroni 10:4 tells us that after pondering the scriptures (studying out in our own minds what we have read), we should ask Heavenly Father "if these things are not true"; and "he will manifest the truth of it unto [us] by the power of the Holy Ghost."

### Conclusion

In order to effectively teach from the scriptures, we must prepare by reading regularly. We must ponder the material by thinking about it, feeling it, and praying with sincere intent. Then we must practice what we have come to know and understand through the Spirit. When we have done this, we can teach from the scriptures with power and persuasion.

### Challenges

As you read the scriptures each day, underline or mark passages that are significant for you. Consider how they can be "likened to us."

Teach your family from the scriptures in family home evening, around the dinner table, or in some other family situations by using scripture stories and applying them to your family's needs.

**Additional Scriptures**

- 2 Nephi 4:15–16 (Nephi's joy in the scriptures)

- Doctrine and Covenants 11:21–22 (we should study before teaching)

- Doctrine and Covenants 42:12–15 (we should teach from the scriptures)

**Teacher Preparation**

Before presenting this lesson:

1. Read *Gospel Principles* chapter 10, "Scriptures."

2. Assign class members to present any stories, scriptures, or quotations you wish.

# TEACHING BY THE POWER OF THE HOLY GHOST

*Lesson   1 8*

The purpose of this lesson is to help us understand that we should teach the gospel by the power of the Holy Ghost.

**Introduction**

Elder Dallin H. Oaks taught: "If we have the Spirit of the Lord to guide us, we can teach any person, no matter how well educated, any place in the world. The Lord knows more than any of us, and if we are his servants, acting under his Spirit, he can deliver his message of salvation to each and every soul" ("Teaching and Learning by the Spirit," *Ensign,* Mar. 1997, 7).

If we are to teach the gospel of Jesus Christ, we must have the guidance of the Holy Ghost. Only in this way can we teach the truth.

**Teaching by the Influence of the Holy Ghost**

- Ask a class member to read Doctrine and Covenants 42:12–14. What does this scripture tell us to teach? Where do we find these principles? How do we obtain the Spirit with which to teach? If we do not have the influence of the Holy Ghost, why should we not teach?

To know what and when to teach, we must learn to recognize the influence of the Holy Ghost. Elder A. Theodore Tuttle explained what it feels like to speak by the power of the Holy Ghost:

"Do you sense when revelation comes? Let me share this experience with you. . . .

". . . Traveling [with Elder Marion G. Romney] to Salt Lake after [a] meeting, one of the Brethren [with us] observed, 'Brother Romney, you spoke under the inspiration of the Holy Ghost tonight.'

"Brother Romney said, 'That's right, I did. Do you know how I know? Because I, too, learned something that I did not know'" ("Teaching the Word to the Rising Generation," address delivered 10 July 1970 at BYU summer school, 8–9).

- How did the Holy Ghost influence President Romney? How can the Holy Ghost increase our ability to teach?

The Holy Ghost not only teaches the teacher, but also causes the words of the teacher to sink deep into the hearts of the listeners. "For when a man speaketh by the power of the Holy Ghost the power of the Holy Ghost carrieth it unto the hearts of the children of men" (2 Nephi 33:1).

- How does the Holy Ghost influence those who are being taught?

- Show visual 18-a, "King Benjamin changed the lives of many people when he taught them by the power of the Holy Ghost."

The Book of Mormon prophet King Benjamin called his people together toward the end of his life to give them special instructions and to strengthen them spiritually.

- Ask a class member to read Mosiah 5:1–2. What caused the people to believe King Benjamin's words? Have a class member read Mosiah 5:3–4. Why were these people so receptive to the influence of the Holy Ghost?

### Obtaining the Guidance of the Holy Ghost

The Book of Mormon tells us that many of the prophets and missionaries of that time were guided in their teaching by the Holy Ghost. Four of these men were the sons of Mosiah.

- Ask a class member to read Alma 17:2–3. What three steps did the sons of Mosiah take to enable them to teach with power?

President Marion G. Romney shared an experience his wife had when she was preparing a lesson she was to teach on the First Vision of the Prophet Joseph Smith. In her class was a well-educated woman who was a nonmember and did not believe in the restored gospel. Sister Romney was an inexperienced teacher at the time and was afraid that her lesson would not be accepted by this intelligent woman.

"[In discussing the problem with her mother, Sister Romney] said, 'Mother, I can't give that lesson. I don't know that Joseph Smith had that vision.' . . .

"Her mother was not an educated woman, but she did have a testimony. She said to her daughter, 'You know how the Prophet got the vision, don't you?'

" 'Yes,' answered her daughter, 'he got it by praying to God for wisdom.' . . .

"The daughter went to her room and tried it; she 'wrestled' with God, as did Enos. The result was that she . . . gave the lesson convincingly,

*18-a, King Benjamin changed the lives of many people when he taught them by the power of the Holy Ghost.*

with power beyond her natural abilities. How could she do it? Well, the Holy Spirit came to her in response to her inquiry. She received a burning within her soul. She knew that Joseph Smith had seen the vision, as well as he knew it. She had not seen exactly the same things with her eyes that the Prophet saw, but she had the same knowledge. She knew from Joseph Smith's description what he had seen, and she had a witness from the Holy Ghost that his account was true" ("How to Gain a Testimony," *New Era*, May 1976, 10–11).

- How did Sister Romney prepare for her lesson? Why didn't studying alone give her confidence to give the lesson?

- Have a class member read Moroni 10:4–5. In what ways does the Holy Ghost help us learn the truth? What do we have to do to receive this witness?

## Testimony Gives Power to Teaching

Teaching with a testimony is teaching with a knowledge that the gospel is true. If we have a testimony of what we are teaching, those listening will feel the power of the Spirit and understand the gospel better. When we bear testimony of the truth, the Holy Ghost witnesses to those listening to us the truthfulness of our testimony (see D&C 50:21–22).

- Show visual 18-b, "The Holy Ghost confirms the testimonies of those who bear witness of gospel truths."

Elder Alvin R. Dyer told the following story about the power of testimony in teaching:

Two missionaries arrived at a home in the late afternoon. The family was just preparing to eat, so the missionaries had little success with their message. As the woman began to close the door, the elders seized the opportunity to bear testimony to the truthfulness of the gospel. One of them purposely raised his voice so that those on the inside could hear. Then, because it had started to rain, the missionaries left rather hurriedly. After traveling about a half a block, they heard someone calling to them. A young man about 14 years of age caught up with them and said, "Father wants you to come back." They went back to the house they had just left. The father told them he had listened to their message at the door. He was not impressed until he heard one of them bear his testimony. Then he said, "A strange feeling came over me, and I knew we had done wrong in sending you away." That testimony, borne by a humble elder, led to the baptism of the family. (See " 'When Thou Art Converted,' " *Instructor*, July 1961, 225.)

*18-b, The Holy Ghost confirms the testimonies of those who bear witness of gospel truths.*

- Why did the father call the missionaries back? Ask the previously assigned class members to describe how they felt the Spirit when they were taught the gospel and heard the testimony of the missionaries.

President Gordon B. Hinckley taught: "The Holy Ghost is the Testifier of Truth, who can teach men things they cannot teach one another. In those great and challenging words of Moroni, a knowledge of the truth of the Book of Mormon is promised 'by the power of the Holy Ghost.' Moroni then declares, 'And by the power of the Holy Ghost ye may know the truth of all things' (Moroni 10:4–5)." (*Teachings of Gordon B. Hinckley* [1997], 259).

## Conclusion

As parents and teachers in the Church, we have a responsibility to teach by the power of the Spirit. When we teach by the Spirit, we increase the knowledge and faith not only of those we teach, but also of ourselves.

Only by teaching with the power of the Holy Ghost can we teach the truth. But to teach by the power of the Holy Ghost, we must be worthy and prepared. Such preparation includes studying, praying, and living the commandments of God.

"And the Spirit shall be given unto you by the prayer of faith; and if ye receive not the Spirit ye shall not teach. . . .

"And as ye shall lift up your voices by the Comforter, ye shall speak and prophesy as seemeth me good;

"For behold, the Comforter knoweth all things" (D&C 42:14, 16–17).

## Challenges

In preparing to teach, seek the guidance of the Holy Ghost by studying the scriptures, praying for guidance, and fasting.

Seek opportunities to teach children, friends, and neighbors.

## Additional Scriptures

- Luke 24:32 (how it feels to be inspired by the Holy Ghost)

- John 14:26 (the Comforter teaches us all things)

- 2 Nephi 32:7–8 (the Spirit encourages us to pray)

- Alma 5:43–52 (fasting and praying encourages guidance from the Holy Ghost)

- Moroni 10:7–10 (gifts from God are received through faith)

## Teacher Preparation

Before presenting this lesson:

1. Follow the steps outlined in the lesson to be influenced by the Holy Ghost as you prepare the lesson.

2. If you desire, assign two class members to describe how they felt the Spirit when they were taught the gospel and heard the testimony of the missionaries.

3. Assign class members to present any stories, scriptures, or quotations you wish.

# TEACHING MODESTY AND VIRTUE IN THE HOME

*Lesson 19*

The purpose of this lesson is to help us know how to teach modesty and virtue in the home.

### Introduction

Elder Boyd K. Packer, in speaking about the moral values of modesty and virtue, said: "The responsibility and the right to teach these sacred [things] rest with the parents in the home. I do not believe that it is the responsibility of the public schools, nor is it the responsibility of the organizations of the Church. The contribution of the Church in this respect is to teach parents the standards of morality that the Lord has revealed and to assist them in their responsibility of teaching these sacred subjects to their children" (*Teach Ye Diligently* [1975], 256).

The prophet Mormon wrote a letter to his son Moroni in which he taught the great value of moral purity. He said that chastity and virtue are more dear and precious than any other thing (see Moroni 9:9). These values are just as important today. Our bodies are sacred; we should always dress modestly and keep ourselves pure and virtuous.

### Modesty and Virtue

The Lord places great value on virtue. It is important, therefore, to understand what the Lord means by modesty and virtue. Modesty usually refers to the way we speak and dress. Virtue refers to the way we act. President Spencer W. Kimball said:

"Another of the many things that lead to unchastity is immodesty. Today many young women and young men are smug in their knowledge of the facts of life. They think they know all the answers. They talk about sex as freely as they talk about cars and shows and clothes. And a spirit of immodesty has developed until nothing seems to be sacred.

"One contributing factor to immodesty and a breakdown of moral values is the modern dress. I am sure that the immodest clothes that are worn by some of our young women, and their mothers, contribute directly and indirectly to the immorality of this age. Even fathers sometimes encourage it. I wonder if our young sisters realize the temptation they are flaunting before young men when they leave their bodies partly uncovered. . . .

"I am positive that the clothes we wear can be a tremendous factor in the gradual breakdown of our love of virtue, our steadfastness in chastity" (*Faith Precedes the Miracle* [1972], 163, 168).

- How should knowing our bodies are sacred affect the way we dress and act? How should knowing we are children of our Heavenly Father affect the way we dress and act?

Elder Vaughn J. Featherstone told a story about the son of a king who understood who he was and how he should act. King Louis XVI of France had been taken from his throne and put in prison. His young son, the prince, was taken by those who had captured the king. Because the young prince was to be the next king, they wanted to destroy him morally. They knew that if they did, he would never be able to become the king of France.

These people took the prince to a faraway city, where they tempted the boy with every filthy thing they could find. They tried to get him to eat foods which would quickly make him lose control of himself. They used terrible language around him all the time. They tempted him with evil women. They exposed him to dishonor and distrust. He was surrounded constantly by everything that could make a person lose his moral values. For over six months he was given this treatment. But not once did the boy give in to temptation. Finally, after doing everything they could think of, they asked why he did not do these things. He replied, "I cannot do what you ask, for I was born to be a king" (adapted from "The King's Son," *New Era*, Nov. 1975, 35).

We too were born to be kings (see 1 Peter 2:9; Revelation 1:6). Our purpose in life, however, is greater than being the king of a nation. We are children of God, and we were born to become like Him. Achieving such a goal is impossible if we are not modest and virtuous.

**The Importance of Example**

One of our most important responsibilities as members of God's Church is to set a proper example of modesty and virtue. We should not only keep our minds and bodies clean and pure, but we should also show that we consider our bodies sacred by the way we talk, the humor we enjoy, and the literature we read. This is especially important for parents and older children. When we set a proper example, our children or our brothers and sisters can develop the same values we have and behave as we behave.

- Have the class members think for a moment about their own attitudes and behaviors and ask themselves the following questions:

  "Is there anything in my attitude and behavior that might be harmful to those I try to teach?"

  "Is there anything that I do or think about that I would not want my children to do or think about?"

- Read Jacob 2:35, which contains Jacob's chastisement of the Nephites for their bad examples. Why is it so important to set the proper example?

**Teaching Modesty and Virtue**

Teaching modesty and virtue requires the guidance of the Spirit. Elder Boyd K. Packer said, "If there is one essential ingredient for the teaching of moral and spiritual values, . . . it is to have the Spirit of the Lord with us as we teach" (*Teach Ye Diligently* [1975], 272).

It is also essential to approach the subject with reverence and humility. Elder Packer's approach is a good example of one way to teach modesty and virtue in a very reverent way:

"There was provided in our physical bodies, and this is sacred, a power of creation. A light, so to speak, that has the power to kindle other lights. This gift is to be used only within the sacred bonds of marriage. Through the exercise of this power of creation, a mortal body may be conceived, a spirit enter into it, and a new soul born into this life.

"This power is good. It can create and sustain family life, and it is in family life that we find the fountains of happiness. It is given to virtually every individual who is born into mortality. It is a sacred and significant power. . . .

"You are growing up in a society where before you is the constant invitation to tamper with these sacred powers. . . . Do not let anyone at all touch or handle your body, not anyone! Those who tell you otherwise proselyte you to share their guilt. We teach you to maintain your innocence. . . . The only righteous use of this sacred power is within the covenant of marriage. Never misuse these sacred powers" (*Teach Ye Diligently* [1975], 259, 262).

If we are to be successful in teaching these principles to our families, we must be very careful to protect our homes against uncleanliness. Elder A. Theodore Tuttle taught us that "the father is the protector of the home. He guards it against the intrusion of evil from without. Formerly he protected his home with weapons and shuttered windows. Today the task is more complex. Barred doors and windows pro-

*19-a, A father should interview his children regularly.*

tect only against [physical things]. It is not an easy thing to protect one's family against intrusions of evil into the minds and spirits of family members. These things can and do flow freely into the home. [Satan is very clever.] He need not break down the door" (in Conference Report, Oct. 1973, 86–87; or *Ensign,* Jan. 1974, 67).

- What are some of the ways that evil can get into our homes today? (Answers could include immoral magazines, radio programs, television shows, books, and the Internet.)

- What can a father do to protect his family from these kinds of things? (Carefully help family members select reading materials, radio and television programs, and materials on the Internet.)

- Read and discuss Doctrine and Covenants 93:40–43.

The Lord chastised Frederick G. Williams because he had not fulfilled his responsibility to bring up his children in light and truth.

- Invite class members to think about how they would feel if the Lord told them they had been unfaithful in teaching their children the importance of modesty and virtue. Invite them also to ponder ways they could improve in teaching their children.

**The Right Time to Teach**

- Show visual 19-a, "A father should interview his children regularly."

Family home evenings are excellent times to teach modesty and virtue. Many fathers also find it helpful to have formal interviews with their children. One father, for example, interviews each child once a month on fast Sunday. He asks questions regarding moral cleanliness and listens to any problems they may have. He teaches, bears his testimony, and tells them of his love for them.

- What effect do you think this kind of interview would have on children?

- Show visual 19-b, "Teaching opportunities often come at unexpected moments."

Although it is vital to teach our children during formal situations such as interviews and family home evenings, we need to be sensitive to their needs at all times. We should watch for the times when they will best understand what we want them to know. If we talk with them regularly and show our love for them, our children will often come to us when they need to talk about their feelings and problems.

*19-b, Teaching opportunities often come at unexpected moments.*

The Lord has commanded us to take advantage of every opportunity to teach our children (see Deuteronomy 6:5–7). If we watch for opportunities to teach, we can sometimes teach very powerfully in very unexpected situations. We may be able to teach important truths about virtue and modesty, for example, on a picnic, after a sacrament meeting, during a walk, in a car, during vacation, on the way to school, or during a time of great difficulty.

▪ Can you think of an experience either with your children or your parents in which real communication and teaching occurred? Where was it? When was it? Was it planned, or did the situation arise unexpectedly?

## Conclusion

We have a responsibility to teach modesty and virtue through our words and our example. As we uphold these values, we will be worthy of the companionship of the Spirit, and we will experience the happiness that comes from being morally clean.

## Challenges

Plan a family home evening to discuss virtue and modesty.

Set an example of modesty and virtue in your own dress and actions.

## Additional Scripture

▪ 1 Timothy 4:12 (the importance of example)

---

## Teacher Preparation

Before presenting this lesson:

1. Carefully plan how you will present the lesson. If there are young priesthood holders in the priesthood class, do not turn the class into a preaching session addressed to them. You may want to discuss with them ways young people can help their parents talk with them about this sensitive subject. Discuss why chastity and modesty are so important and what the class members can do to set a good example for others.

2. Assign class members to present any stories, scriptures, or quotations you wish.

# SETTLING FAMILY PROBLEMS HARMONIOUSLY

*Lesson 20*

---

The purpose of this lesson is to encourage us to settle family difficulties harmoniously in order to build a happy home life.

## Introduction

▪ Show visual 20-a, "Love is the foundation of harmonious family life."

President Joseph F. Smith taught what we must do if we are to have ideal homes:

"What . . . is an ideal home . . . ? It is one . . . in which the father is devoted to the family with which God has blessed him, counting them of first importance, and in which they in turn permit him to live in their hearts. One in which there is confidence, union, love, sacred devotion between father and mother and children and parents" (*Gospel Doctrine*, 5th ed. [1939], 302–3).

Although all of us are trying to achieve ideal homes, we all occasionally experience conflicts. Even the Prophet Joseph Smith felt disharmony in his home at times. One morning, for example, when he was translating the Book of Mormon, he became upset about something his wife had done. Later, as he tried to translate some of the Book of Mormon, he found he could not. He went to an orchard and prayed, and when he came back he asked for Emma's forgiveness. Only then was he able to translate. (See B. H. Roberts, *A Comprehensive History of the Church*, 1:131.)

The Lord also expects us to recognize the sources of disharmony in our homes and to solve our problems harmoniously.

## Sources of Disharmony in Our Homes

The scriptures tell us that Satan's influence is a major cause of disharmony and contention.

▪ Read 3 Nephi 11:29–30. How does Satan "[stir] up the hearts of men to contend with anger"?

*20-a, Love is the foundation of harmonious family life.*

Whenever the spirit of contention comes into our homes, the Spirit of the Lord will leave. And without the Spirit of the Lord in our homes, we cannot be happy and feel the joy of the Lord and His gospel.

Our own personal weaknesses may also cause contention with others (see James 4:1). When a person is not at peace with himself, it is very difficult to live in harmony with others. Among the weaknesses that can cause disharmony are lust, greed, impure desires, and conflicting loyalties. President Spencer W. Kimball mentioned one weakness in particular: "A couple may have poverty, illness, disappointment, failures, and even death in the family, but these will not rob them of their peace. The marriage can be successful so long as selfishness does not enter in. Troubles and problems will draw [partners] together into unbreakable unions if there is total unselfishness there" (*Marriage and Divorce* [1976], 19, 22).

- Why is selfishness such a source of disharmony and unhappiness in the home?

As President Kimball mentioned, problems that are commonly thought to cause unhappiness, such as poverty and illness, can actually bring a family closer together if family members work together unselfishly and lovingly.

**Dealing with Family Problems**

The following are ways the Lord and our Church leaders have given us to prevent or solve family problems.

*Accept Responsibility*

Parents and children both have responsibilities to each other.

- Read about some of these responsibilities in Ephesians 6:1–4. What duty does a young man have to his parents? What duties do parents have to their children? How will accepting these responsibilities help to promote harmony in the home?

*Avoid Unkind Words*

Angry, unkind words have no place in our homes. Elder Boyd K. Packer counseled: "As you enter the marriage covenant, [you should never speak] a cross word—not one. It is neither necessary nor desirable. There are many who teach that it is normal and expected for domestic difficulty and bickering and strife to be a part of that marriage relationship. . . . I know that it is possible to live together in love with never the first cross word ever passing between you" (*Eternal Marriage*, Brigham Young University Speeches of the Year [14 Apr. 1970], 6). A soft, understanding answer calms us; angry words only cause more conflict (see Proverbs 15:1).

- What is the difference between discussing differences and arguing?

*Admit Mistakes*

President Spencer W. Kimball gave this counsel:

"Being human, you may some day have differences of opinion resulting even in little quarrels. . . . Suppose an injury has been inflicted; unkind words have been said; hearts are torn; and each feels that the other is wholly at fault. Nothing is done to heal the wound. The hours pass. There is a throbbing of hearts through the night, a day of sullenness and unkindness and further misunderstanding. Injury is heaped upon injury until the attorney is employed, the home broken, and the lives of the parents and children blasted.

"But there is a healing balm which, if applied early, in but a few minutes will return you to [proper] thinking; . . . with so much at stake— your love, yourselves, your family, your ideals, your exaltation, your eternities—you cannot afford to take chances. You must swallow your pride and with courage, [say to your wife:] 'Darling, I'm sorry. I didn't mean to hurt you. Please forgive me.' And [your wife will reply:] 'Dear, it was I who was at fault more than you. Please forgive me.' And you go into one another's arms and life [will be good] again. And when you retire at night, it is forgotten, and there is no chasm between you as you have your family prayer" (*Faith Precedes the Miracle* [1972], 134).

- What are some things that cause misunderstandings and quarrels? How can identifying the causes of the problems help us solve them? Why is it so difficult to admit our mistakes?

President Spencer W. Kimball told us to admit our mistakes and to say "I'm sorry." When we sincerely do this, we have taken a large step toward settling family disharmony. Parents need to do this with their children too, not just with each other.

*Show Kindness*

One of the principles the scriptures give us to help us make our home life happier is kindness. We are commanded, in fact, to be kind, loving, and forgiving. Both children and adults in a family are counseled to treat each other with respect and the type of kindness Christ has shown us. In these matters, we should always let Christ be our model. (See Ephesians 4:29–32.)

- Ask the assigned Aaronic Priesthood bearer to tell what things a young man can do to help promote harmony in the home.

President Spencer W. Kimball taught us how to achieve family happiness: "You ask, 'What is the price of happiness?' You will be surprised with the simplicity of the answer. The treasure house of happiness may be unlocked and remain open to those who use the following keys: First, you must live the gospel of Jesus Christ in its purity and simplicity. . . . Second, you must forget yourself and love your companion more than yourself. If you do these things, happiness will be yours in great and never failing abundance" (*Faith Precedes the Miracle* [1972], 126).

▪ How can kindness prevent and solve family problems?

*Pray*

Harmony in the home is encouraged when we ask the Lord in family and personal prayer to help us overcome our differences.

▪ Read 3 Nephi 18:19–21. Notice that it is a duty to pray in our families. How does prayer help to solve family problems?

The following story tells how one mother prayed for guidance to solve a problem in her home:

"It was about a week after we had taken ten-year-old Wayne into our home through the Church Indian Placement Program. He was a bright, handsome little boy, but, of course, he had to prove himself to the other boys. He fought with them quite often, and he could hold his own with the best of them.

"One day I received a phone call from his school teacher. The teacher informed me that he was having trouble with Wayne at school. Wayne was disrespectful to him and to other teachers. This was a blow to me. I had never had a problem like that with my own children, and it greatly upset me. Of course my temper flared, as it so often does, and I began to rehearse all the things I was going to tell Wayne when he returned home from school. 'I must nip this problem in the bud,' I told myself.

"To make matters worse, Wayne was late coming home from school because of a fight with a neighbor boy. They fought all the way from the bus stop. Finally they were on our front lawn. Both of them were fighting rough. I watched for awhile, until I was sure that the fight was indeed serious, then I stepped to the door and called Wayne into the house.

"He ignored me. He was not about to back down from the other boy. As I watched, I became even more angry. I *ordered* Wayne into the house. I was so angry that I knew I could not deal with the problem while in that state, so I sent him into his room to read.

"Shaking with anger, I slipped into my own bedroom and knelt and prayed. I prayed for wisdom in handling the problem, and I also asked that through the Spirit I would know what to say. As I stood up after praying, I felt a warm, calm feeling consume me. It started at my head and gently flowed to my feet.

"As I opened the door to Wayne's room and saw him sitting there on the edge of the bed with a book in his hands, a million thoughts raced through my mind. He looked so out of place sitting in that room; somehow he belonged outdoors where he could run free, as he was used to doing. In an instant my heart went out to this little fellow so all alone, a little boy uprooted from familiar surroundings and plopped down in a different world, to live by different rules. He had to prove to the other boys that he was just as good, if not better, than they.

"I sat on the edge of the bed next to him, and put my arm around his shoulders. The first words I spoke surprised even me, for I said, 'Wayne, forgive me for being so cross with you.' Then I told him of the phone call from his teacher and gave him an opportunity to explain himself. We had a wonderful talk; he confided in me, and as we spoke, we did so in whispers. This was much different from the tone I had expected to use before asking my Heavenly Father for help. It was a truly spiritual experience and it did more for the relationship between Wayne and me than any other thing.

"Thank goodness we have prayer and the gift of the Holy Spirit to guide us if we ask for it" (Myrna Behunin, "We Talked in Whispers," *Ensign,* Jan. 1976, 51–52).

### Conclusion

Challenges occur in the life of every family. We can choose how we will meet and resolve these challenges. By practicing the righteous principles discussed in this lesson, we can resolve challenges in our families and increase in love and unity.

Have class members sing "Love at Home" (*Hymns*, no. 294; or *Gospel Principles,* 352) at the close of the class.

### Challenges

Build and improve the happiness of your own home by identifying any sources of disharmony among the family members.

If you have had unkind words with a family member, admit your mistake.

Treat family members with kindness.

### Additional Scriptures

- Matthew 7:12 (our relationship with others)

- Galatians 5:22 (the fruit of the Spirit)

- Doctrine and Covenants 88:119–26 (counsel from the Lord to members of the Church)

**Teacher Preparation**

Before presenting this lesson:

1. Read *Gospel Principles* chapter 36, "The Family Can Be Eternal."

2. Assign an Aaronic Priesthood bearer to tell how young men can promote harmony in the home.

3. Assign class members to present any stories, scriptures, or quotations you wish.

# MANAGING FAMILY FINANCES

*Lesson  2 1*

The purpose of this lesson is to help us learn and apply the basic principles of wise money management.

## Introduction

Of the numerous references in the scriptures to money and riches, many warn us not to covet wealth. For this reason, many people fear that all money is evil and that they may displease the Lord if they spend time and energy in earning and saving money. But this is not true. It is the *love* of money that is "the root of all evil," not money itself (see 1 Timothy 6:10).

President Spencer W. Kimball said: "Not all money is filthy. There is clean money—clean money with which to buy food, clothes, and shelter, and with which to make contributions." President Kimball went on to explain that "clean money" is the pay we receive for honest work. He said that money becomes filthy only when it is obtained from any type of dishonesty. (See *Faith Precedes the Miracle* [1972], 235–36.)

Neither wealth nor poverty is an indication of individual worthiness. Some great men of God have been rich and some have been poor. The amount of money we have is not important, but rather how we obtain and use it. Using money to provide for the temporal needs of our families, for example, is not only proper, but is a commandment from God (see 1 Timothy 5:8). The commandment to provide for our families is easier to obey when we learn and apply the basic principles of wise money management.

## Principles of Wise Money Management

Although everything on the earth belongs to the Lord (see Psalm 24:1), He allows us to use and possess some of His earthly things. We are warned, however, that the Lord will hold us accountable for how we manage what He has permitted us to use. In the parable of the talents, for example, the Savior teaches us the importance of wisely managing our earthly possessions.

- Ask a class member to read the parable of the talents found in Matthew 25:14–30. (In the days of Jesus, a talent was a unit of money.)

There are several basic principles we should consider in managing our money wisely. Almost all of us can improve in one or more of these areas. The Lord will help us improve as we put Him first and follow the principles of wise money management.

- List each principle of wise money management on the chalkboard as it is discussed.

### Pay Tithes and Offerings

The first and most important payment we should make is tithing. The Lord has promised those who pay their tithing faithfully that He will "open . . . the windows of heaven, and pour . . . out a blessing, that there shall not be room enough to receive it" (Malachi 3:10). Although the Lord does not promise us great wealth if we pay our tithes and offerings, He does promise to bless us both spiritually and temporally.

### Work

Work is a blessing that allows us to provide for our families. By work-ing steadily and honestly, we can attain financial security. (Lesson 23 of this manual contains counsel on developing and improving our employment skills.)

### Avoid Unnecessary Debt

Although it is sometimes necessary to borrow money, we should avoid debt as much as possible. We should pay off the debts we have as quickly as possible. Elder Ezra Taft Benson said: "Let us live within our income. Let us pay as we go. . . . Let us heed the counsel of the leader-ship of the Church. Get out of debt!" (*Pay Thy Debt and Live*, Brigham Young University Speeches of the Year [28 Feb. 1962], 12).

- How can we avoid unnecessary debt?

### Plan and Spend Carefully

- Read Luke 14:28. What does it mean to "count the cost"?

As this scripture tells us, we must plan carefully before spending our money. Many people get into debt because they fail to control their spending. If a family plans how to use their money, they will keep out of financial trouble.

We need to consider carefully the importance of each purchase before we make it. Many things we buy are actually of no value to ourselves or our families. If we take time to think about the future use of any item before we buy it, we will avoid buying things we really do not need.

- Read 2 Nephi 9:51. What are some of the things of "no worth" for which we are tempted to spend our money?

*Save*

For many people, saving money is very difficult. As members of the Church, we have been counseled to regularly save a portion of our income. If we make up our minds to regularly save even a small part of our earnings, whether they be money or materials, we will someday be glad we did so. In setting up a savings program, we are providing financial security for our families as we plan for the future. We can also save for a special purpose, such as going on a mission or traveling to the temple.

### Using Family Councils to Manage Money

Too often, we spend as much money as we earn. Our wants seem to increase as fast or faster than our income. It is very important, therefore, that we budget our money carefully. Although each family differs in its needs and wants, most families find it helpful to follow a plan similar to the one described below:

- Show visual 21-a, "Family council is a good time to make a budget."

All members of the family should discuss financial matters and agree on a system for handling finances. This may be done by holding a family council in which the father presides and family members participate. At this council, the family should make a list of all sources of income for family use. This list might include money earned by members of the family, homegrown vegetables and grains that could be sold, or items made at home to sell to others.

Next, the family should write down all their needs and wants, listing first the more important expenses and then the desired but nonessential items. The list might include Church contributions; savings (for such things as going to the temple, serving a mission, and gaining an education); taxes; and money budgeted for housing, food, clothing, tools, transportation, and recreation.

Finally, the family should agree on how much money can be set aside for each item. Some less important items at the end of the list may never be purchased, but it is better to take care of the necessities first. President Brigham Young once said: "Our wants are many, but our real necessities are very few. Let us govern our wants by our necessities, and we shall find that we are not compelled to spend our money for naught" (*Discourses of Brigham Young* [1954], 297). On another occasion he explained that poverty is caused by the lack of wise judgment. He noted that many people who earn very little waste it on unimportant

*21-a, Family council is a good time to make a budget.*

things until they are deeply in debt. (See *Discourses of Brigham Young* [1954], 317.)

- Show visual 21-b, "A sample budget." Explain that a family could use a list like this to plan a budget in family council.

We will be blessed greatly as we plan carefully and budget our money. Setting goals, making plans, and working together to achieve them will allow us to take care of our families as the Lord has commanded. An added blessing from working together is the greater love and unity our families will enjoy. The following story shows how a man (Vaha'i Tonga) and his family were blessed as they worked and budgeted together:

"I promised our four children that if they would help, we could go to the temple together. I thought to myself, 'How can you say, be a good boy or be a good girl, if I am not sealed to them in the temple?' I had the feeling that they were not mine.

"For two years we sacrificed almost everything. I divided my pay from school for each one of us, and we saved that. But we paid our tithing and fast offerings. We were left with 70¢ in our hands each month. This is how I lived with my family, on 70¢ a month for two years. We lived on what we could grow and gather. I remember my wife would wake up early in the morning to make our salads with bananas and coconut milk. My children could not buy candy or shoes or go to movies because they were saving to go to the temple. . . .

"Through sacrifice we were able to take our family to New Zealand to be sealed in the temple. We had to do some extra things to accomplish our goals, but it was a great blessing to us" ("We Lived on 70 Cents a Month for the Temple," *Ensign*, Feb. 1976, 31).

### Conclusion

Our Heavenly Father has counseled us to manage our money so we can care for our families and be happy. If we do not care for our families, the Lord will hold us accountable. In order to care for our families, we should follow the basic steps and guiding principles of wise money management. If we put spiritual things first, the Lord will help us manage our finances.

### Challenge

Analyze your spending practices, and set up a workable budget by following the principles outlined in the lesson.

### Additional Scriptures

- Proverbs 22:7 (the borrower is servant to the lender)

# Budget

**Total income**                    _____

Tithing—10 percent              _____

Church contributions          _____

Savings                              _____

Food                                  _____

Clothing                            _____

Housing                            _____

Medical expenses              _____

Transportation                  _____

Utilities                            _____

Other                                _____

Other                                _____

Other                                _____

**Total expenses**                 _____

*21-b, A sample budget.*

- Malachi 3:8–11 (payment of tithes and offerings brings blessings)

- Jacob 2:18–19 (we should seek the kingdom of God before seeking riches)

- Doctrine and Covenants 56:16–17 (warnings to the rich and to the poor)

- Doctrine and Covenants 104:11–13 (all men are accountable for stewardships over earthly blessings)

**Teacher Preparation**

Before presenting this lesson:

1. Read *Gospel Principles* chapter 27, "Work and Personal Responsibility."

2. Read chapter 23, "Developing and Improving Employment Skills," in this manual.

3. Assign a class member to tell the parable of the talents (see Matthew 25:14–30).

4. Assign class members to present any stories, scriptures, or quotations you wish.

# HOME PRODUCTION
# AND STORAGE

---

The purpose of this lesson is to help us understand and apply the essentials of home production and storage.

### Introduction

Church leaders have counseled all Latter-day Saints to become self-reliant and independent. There are good reasons for this counsel. President Marion G. Romney explained that "we're living in the latter days. . . . We are living in the era just preceding the second [coming] of the Lord Jesus Christ. We are told to so prepare and live that we can be . . . independent of every other creature beneath the celestial kingdom" (in Conference Report, Apr. 1975, 165; see also D&C 78:13–14).

- Display visual 22-a, "Disaster may strike when we least expect it."

President Spencer W. Kimball encouraged us to become self-reliant because the prophecies of old are coming to pass. He said: "Now I think the time is coming when there will be more distresses, when there may be more tornadoes and more floods, . . . more earthquakes. . . . I think they will be increasing probably as we come nearer to the end, and so we must be prepared for this" (in Conference Report, Apr. 1974, 184).

He also said: "Should evil times come, many might wish they had filled all their fruit bottles and cultivated a garden in their backyards and planted a few fruit trees and berry bushes and provided for their own commodity needs. The Lord planned that we would be independent of every creature, but we note even many farmers buy their milk from dairies and home owners buy their garden vegetables from the store. And should the trucks fail to fill the shelves of the stores, many would go hungry" (in Conference Report, Oct. 1974, 6; or *Ensign*, Nov. 1974, 6).

- Have the brethren imagine that the stores were closed and that they had to rely on their own supplies for everything. Ask them what they would like to have or be producing at home if those imaginary conditions had just occurred.

*22-a, Disaster may strike when we least expect it.*

**Providing for Our Own Needs**

President Kimball instructed us to "study the best methods of providing your own foods. . . . If there are children in your home, involve them in the process with assigned responsibilities" (in Conference Report, Apr. 1976, 170–71; or *Ensign*, May 1976, 124).

Bishop Vaughn J. Featherstone told us which skills we should develop if we are to provide for our needs: "Now regarding home production: Raise animals where means and local laws permit. Plant fruit trees, grapevines, berry bushes, and vegetables. You will provide food for your family, much of which can be eaten fresh. Other food you grow can be preserved and included as part of your home storage. Wherever possible, produce your nonfood necessities of life. . . . Make or build needed items. I might also add, beautify, repair, and maintain all of your property" ("Food Storage," *Ensign*, May 1976, 117).

▪ Display a poster of the following list, or write the information on the chalkboard:

---

a. Raise livestock.

b. Plant fruit trees, berry bushes, and grapevines.

c. Plant vegetable gardens.

d. Preserve and store food.

e. Make or build needed items.

f. Repair and maintain property.

---

*Raise Livestock*

▪ Display visual 22-b, "Chickens are easy to raise and care for."

If we have enough land and live where we can legally keep livestock, we should buy and raise some animals. Before we decide which animals we will raise, however, we must be prepared to care for them properly. This means learning about the food, shelter, and care they need in order to be healthy. Some animals that are easy to care for are chickens, rabbits, ducks, and milk goats.

▪ Discuss the kinds of livestock most commonly raised in the area. Discuss the kinds of food, shelter, and care that each animal requires.

*Plant Fruit Trees, Berry Bushes, and Grapevines*

Because fruit trees, bushes, and vines bear fruit either every year or every other year, they do not need to be planted again each year, as do

*22-b, Chickens are easy to raise and care for.*

vegetables. They may not bear fruit, however, for several years after they are planted, so we should plant them as soon as possible if we are to have the fruit when we most need it. Before we plant them, we should learn how much space each tree or bush will require when it is fully grown as well as how to care for it properly.

- Discuss what kinds of fruit trees, vines, and berry bushes produce well in the area. Discuss the kind of care each one needs.

### Plant Vegetable Gardens

- Display visual 22-c, "Every family should plant a vegetable garden."

Church leaders have counseled every family in the Church to have a vegetable garden. Even if we do not save money on the project, each family needs to learn how to provide for themselves. A garden supplies fresh food as well as extra food that we can preserve and store.

### Preserve and Store Food

In some countries there are laws against storing food. President Kimball said that those who live in these countries should honor, obey, and sustain the laws of the country and should not store food (see Conference Report, Apr. 1976, 170; or *Ensign*, May 1976, 124). But where it is permitted, we should follow the counsel of the Lord to store food in case there comes a time when there is no other food available. When a hurricane hit Honduras in the fall of 1974, the members of the Church there who had dried and stored their own food were grateful they had done so. Only a few months before the hurricane, the mission president had warned them of impending disaster, challenging them to begin a food storage program. The beans, flour, rice, and other food they had put away saved the Saints from hunger. (See Bruce B. Chapman, "Hurricane in Honduras," *New Era*, Jan. 1975, 31.)

There are several ways to preserve and store our own food. We can:

1. Store it in the ground. This method is good for some root vegetables and certain green, leafy vegetables if the place we store them is cool and dry. Too much rain or poor drainage will ruin them.

2. Dry it. When there is a period of warm, sunny weather, fruits and vegetables can be dried in the sun. They must be covered or brought inside when it rains. Produce may also be dried in a dehydrator.

3. Bottle it. This method is simple, but dangerous if done improperly. If done properly, bottling is a good way to store food and maintain its flavor. Proper bottling requires at least a cold-pack canner. (The equipment involved could be shared among several families.) This method also requires that the bottles be protected from breakage.

*22-c, Every family should plant a vegetable garden.*

4. Salt or brine it. This is an inexpensive method of preserving fruits, vegetables, and meat, and requires little or no equipment.

### Make or Build Needed Items

If we had to face a natural disaster, we would need to be prepared to cook, heat our homes, and clean our clothing, our bodies, and our surroundings. For this reason, it is important that we either store fuel and soap, or that we learn to make them in an emergency. Also of importance are first aid articles, prescribed medicines, soaps and other cleaning items, candles, matches, and any other articles necessary for the welfare of the family. Whenever possible, we should not only store these items, but also learn to produce them.

### Repair and Maintain Property

In an emergency, we might also face the need to rebuild our homes, barns, or corrals. It is important, therefore, that members of our families learn to work with wood and other building materials and learn to use tools so they can make and repair furniture and other needed items. When we learn to repair and maintain our own possessions, we can save time and money and avoid being dependent on others.

▪ Why is it important to keep our possessions in good condition?

### Learning New Skills

Some of us have learned skills that we can teach to others. We can also learn skills from books or magazines, classes, government workers, or school programs.

▪ Ask class members to discuss skills they can teach to others. Where are there people who can teach us those skills that we would like to learn? Which classes should we encourage our children to take in school in order to learn useful skills? How can we encourage our families to learn these skills?

### Conclusion

Problems such as financial difficulties or natural disasters are part of our experiences on earth. If we learn to provide for our own needs, we will not fear hard times because we will be prepared. The Lord said, "If ye are prepared ye shall not fear" (D&C 38:30).

### Challenges

Set aside a time this week to talk to your wife and family about home production and storage.

Determine what you will need for a year's supply.

Develop a plan to meet the needs of your family by starting or continuing a garden, learning a skill, or working on another project.

**Teacher Preparation**

Before presenting this lesson:

1. Check with government extension workers or experienced people to:

    a. Find out what kinds of livestock are raised in your area and which are easiest to care for.

    b. Find out which fruit trees, vines, and bushes grow well in the area and what kind of care they need.

    c. Find out if there are classes available that can teach family members how to build housing, furniture, and other needed items. If there are no classes available, find people with these skills who would be willing to teach them.

2. Prepare the poster suggested in the lesson, or write the information on the chalkboard.

3. Assign class members to present any stories, scriptures, or quotations you wish.

# DEVELOPING AND IMPROVING EMPLOYMENT SKILLS

*Lesson 23*

The purpose of this lesson is to help us understand the importance of work, how to wisely select employment, and how to improve our work skills.

### Introduction

The first recorded instruction given to Adam after the Fall was the eternal principle of work. The Lord told Adam, "In the sweat of thy face shalt thou eat bread, till thou return unto the ground" (Genesis 3:19).

Our Heavenly Father has given us this same commandment. The First Presidency of the Church declared, "It is a blessing that we are required to work, and we should do it willingly and without complaint" ("First Presidency Urges Frugality," *Ensign,* Mar. 1975, 75). Work is one of the keys to eternal life. Our wise and loving Heavenly Father knows that we will learn more, grow more, achieve more, and benefit more from a life of work than from a life of ease.

- Show visual 23-a, "Work is a blessing given to us by our Heavenly Father."

### Wise Selection of Employment

Choosing our occupations is very important. We must gather facts, make prayerful decisions, gain training and experience, and then search for employment that will enable us to provide for our families.

### *Gather Facts*

When we are young we should determine the kind of employment that would be best for us by considering our talents, abilities, and interests. We will probably be more successful if we do something we enjoy. Although some of us who already have jobs were not able to choose our employment, we can follow the same steps to improve our employment situation.

Before deciding on an occupation, we should consider the future and security of the job. With the constant changes in the world, many jobs

*23-a, Work is a blessing given to us by our Heavenly Father.*

cease to exist and others are created. One way we can learn about the future of a job we are considering is by seeking the counsel of friends, relatives, fellow priesthood brethren, and Church leaders. In some cities there are employment counselors and agencies that can help. Often, trade schools, high schools, and universities can tell us which jobs are available. If newspapers are available, the "Help Wanted" section can indicate which jobs are in demand.

When choosing a job, we should look for one that will help us keep close to the Church and our families. There are some jobs that may require us to be away from home for long periods of time or offer working conditions that may prevent us from living the gospel as fully as we should. Such conditions can be avoided by choosing our jobs carefully. If we find ourselves in an unsatisfactory job situation, we can work to qualify ourselves for another job.

### Pray

- Show visual 23-b, "The Lord will confirm our choice of employment if we ask Him."

It is very important that we seek the Lord's help when looking for employment. The decisions are ours to make, but the Lord will help us choose wisely if we pray earnestly. But prayer alone is not sufficient. President Brigham Young said: "My faith does not lead me to think the Lord will provide us with roast pigs, [and] bread already buttered . . . ; he will give us the ability to raise the grain, to obtain the fruits of the earth, to make habitations" (*Discourses of Brigham Young* [1954], 291).

- How does President Young's statement relate to finding a job?

As we make our final decision, we need to pray and receive the peace of mind that comes when we know we are being guided by the Holy Ghost. Then we need to act on our decision. The following story shows how Brother Taisho Komura of Japan used these principles to change his life and employment:

Taisho Komura was employed as a barber in Japan. One day he was contacted by the missionaries and later baptized.

During their discussions, he had learned about keeping the Sabbath day holy. The Sabbath, however, was his busiest day in the barber shop. So, after praying about his employment situation, he decided to enter school to change his occupation.

- Have several class members relate how prayer has helped them make good decisions about employment.

*23-b, The Lord will confirm our choice of employment if we ask Him.*

*Develop Employment Skills*

- Show visual 23-c, "Developing a skill requires time and effort."

Developing employment skills requires time and effort. If we want to improve our employment situation, we must be willing to study and work to gain the necessary skill and training.

Apprenticeships, correspondence courses, inservice classes, vocational schools, manuals, and books can all help us develop our skills. Interviewing with potential employers, visiting work locations, and actually working at different jobs will also increase our knowledge and skills.

Reading and writing are two basic skills that will help in obtaining employment. If we are seeking employment and cannot read or write, we should ask help from someone who can. We should never hesitate to use the knowledge and information available from our families, Church members, and the community.

- What skills and talents can each of us share with our brethren in the quorum?

- Have the previously assigned person report on the employment services available in the area.

When we have a goal to achieve, we must be willing to make personal sacrifices to reach it. This means being willing to do all that is necessary to develop our skills. Success comes only if we fulfill the requirements and make the necessary efforts to achieve it. "For whatsoever a man soweth, that shall he also reap" (Galatians 6:7).

The following story shows how a member of the Church in the South Pacific succeeded in his efforts to improve his employment skills and provide for his family.

As a young man, Viliami Havili had learned the importance of individual effort in learning and improving skills that would enable him to provide for his future family. When he did get married, Brother Havili worked hard to earn and save enough money to buy some farmland offered at a low price.

The farmland he bought was thought to be of little value because it was on hilly ground and near the ocean, where the winds could easily destroy the crops. But he worked very hard to prepare the ground for planting. He also spent much time studying all of the latest farming techniques. Because some of the information he needed to know was available only in French books, he taught himself French well enough to read what they taught about agriculture.

*23-c, Developing a skill requires time and effort.*

From these books, he learned how to fertilize the soil, which many other farmers in the area had never bothered to learn. He learned how to use certain chemicals to kill insects and to cure plant diseases. He also found out which crops were selling and being exported for higher prices. Not surprisingly, through his many efforts and with the Lord's help, Brother Havili became a successful farmer.

Like Brother Havili, we can be successful in our employment when we prepare ourselves with the necessary skills.

### Search for Employment

A qualified person cannot be hired until he makes contact with a potential employer. Nor can a man who plans to be self-employed sell his products or services until he makes contact with possible buyers. If we are unemployed, we have the responsibility to actively look for work.

If a priesthood leader finds it difficult to locate work, he may need to obtain help from his priesthood quorum. As quorum members, we can be a resource for each other in searching for employment. We can also obtain help from our stake or ward employment specialist. Members who have questions about the services available through the Church can ask their quorum leader or bishop.

- What are some of the possibilities for employment in our area? What can we do as quorum members to help each other find work?

### Improving Work Habits

The Apostle Paul counseled the brethren of the Church to be "not slothful in business" (Romans 12:11). We should always try our best and look for ways to improve our work habits. To do this, we must have good attitudes about work. The following checklist may help us to keep some of the more important work habits in mind.

Do I use my time well?

Do I cooperate with my employer, my supervisor, and my fellow employees?

Am I using the supplies or property of my employer for personal use without permission or without paying for them?

Could I be more prompt in coming to work and returning from rest periods?

Am I performing my job in the best way I know?

Am I pleasant with my fellow employees, supervisor, and employer?

The following story shows how one of our Church leaders was blessed by improving his work skills:

President Heber J. Grant learned when he was a teenager the importance of improving work skills and putting forth extra effort. One day when he was playing marbles with some other boys they saw a bank bookkeeper. One of the boys remarked, "That man gets $150.00 a month." Heber figured to himself that he would have to shine 120 pairs of shoes every day for a month to make that much money. So he there and then resolved that someday he would be a bookkeeper for a bank.

In those days all records and accounts of banks were written with a pen, and one of the requirements of a good bookkeeper was the ability to write well. To get this job, Heber first practiced his penmanship.

At the beginning, his penmanship was so poor that his friends would make fun of it. This touched his pride, and he said, "I'll some day be able to give you fellows lessons in penmanship." Because of his efforts to develop this skill, he became a teacher of penmanship at a university. He wrote greeting cards, wedding cards, insurance policies, stock certificates, and legal documents.

He said, "I once made $20.00 on New Year's Day by writing forty dozen cards with (Happy New Year) and a man's name in the corner. . . . When [the next] New Year's Eve arrived, I was in the office quite late writing calling cards. Mr. Wadsworth [the boss] came in and pleasantly remarked that business was good. . . . He referred to my having kept the books [for another company] without compensation. He said a number of complimentary things which made me very happy. He then handed me . . . $100.00 which doubly compensated me for all my extra work. The satisfaction enjoyed in feeling that I had won the good will and confidence of my employer was worth more to me than twice $100.00." (See Bryant S. Hinckley, *Heber J. Grant: Highlights in the Life of a Great Leader* [1951], 39–42.)

**Conclusion**

The ability to work is a blessing. The Lord has told us through His prophets that it is our responsibility to work and provide for our families. We can learn good work habits and skills from practice as well as from those who have had experience. To find a job that is rewarding, we should gather the facts, pray about our decisions, and develop employment skills.

**Challenge**

Make a plan to improve in one of the areas mentioned in the personal checklist of work habits found in this chapter.

**Additional Scriptures**

- Doctrine and Covenants 31:5 (the laborer is worthy of his hire)

- Doctrine and Covenants 42:42 (the idle shall not have the blessings of the worker)

---

**Teacher Preparation**

Before presenting this lesson:

1. Read *Gospel Principles* chapter 27, "Work and Personal Responsibility."

2. Review lesson 12, "The Father's Responsibility for the Welfare of His Family," in this manual.

3. Ask a class member to find out what schools and services are available in the area for improving work opportunities and skills. If your ward or stake has an employment specialist, you could ask him or her to present this material.

4. Assign class members to present any stories, scriptures, or quotations you wish.

# KEEPING PHYSICALLY HEALTHY

*L e s s o n    2 4*

---

The purpose of this lesson is to help us understand why it is so important to keep our bodies physically healthy.

**Introduction**

One reason we came to earth was to gain physical bodies. President Brigham Young declared, "Our mortal bodies are all important to us; without them we never can be glorified in the eternities that will be" (*Discourses of Brigham Young* [1954], 56).

Although our bodies will be glorified in eternity (see Alma 11:42–44), in this life they suffer from sickness, disease, pain, and injury. Some are temporarily handicapped. Others are crippled for life. But whatever their condition, our bodies are important to us because they help us progress toward perfection.

Man is both a spiritual and physical being; the physical and spiritual cannot be separated. Our spirits cannot reach their full potential without the support and strength of the body (see D&C 93:33–34). We should develop ourselves spiritually and intellectually, but also remember to develop ourselves physically.

President David O. McKay stated: "The healthy man, who takes care of his physical being, has strength and vitality; his temple is a fit place for his spirit to reside. . . . It is necessary, therefore, to care for our physical bodies, and to observe the laws of physical health and happiness" ("The 'Whole' Man," *Improvement Era*, Apr. 1952, 221).

**The Benefits of Health**

The following are some of the benefits of having a healthy body:

*We Are Able to Serve Better*

The healthier we are, the more capable we are of serving others and bringing happiness to them and ourselves.

*We Are Better Leaders*

Because leaders need strength and energy to fulfill their callings, they need to be as healthy as possible.

*We Feel Better about Ourselves and Others*

When we keep our bodies healthy, we feel good about ourselves and have enthusiasm for our work. We also have more patience, love, and kindness for others.

*We Are Able to Provide for Ourselves and Our Families*

The healthier our bodies are, the better able we are to work and thus provide for ourselves and our families.

## Maintaining Physical Health

Many health problems result from unclean living conditions, disease, excess weight, poor diet, fatigue, and lack of exercise. Regardless of where we live, we may be affected by these health problems. To prevent or solve these health problems, we must first realize what our personal health problems are. Once we have learned this, we can develop programs suited to our schedules which will help us to maintain healthy bodies. A local health center may have helpful information on setting up a health program.

Our personal and family health program should include the following:

*Obedience to the Word of Wisdom*

The Lord has told us that there are certain substances we should not take into our bodies. These include tobacco, coffee, tea, alcohol, drugs, and certain foods. On the other hand, He has suggested some foods and drinks we should use to maintain good healthy bodies. Those who keep the Word of Wisdom are promised health, wisdom, and protection (see D&C 89:18–21).

- Have a class member report on the contents of the Word of Wisdom, found in Doctrine and Covenants 89:1–17.

The following story illustrates some of the blessings that come from obeying the Word of Wisdom.

"I wasn't quite 12 years old, but I worked right alongside my father in the grain harvest over 60 years ago. He cut and I bundled the grain into [bundles]; it was exhausting labor, day after day.

"One Saturday, we began [working] at daylight and stopped about 8:30 that night. I was so tired I wanted to lie down and sleep without even waiting for supper.

*24-a, Regular physical exercise is necessary for good health.*

"My father looked at me and said gently, 'Lee, the patch of grain I cut today was very green. If we wait until Monday to [bundle] it, the kernels will be shrunken. We must do it tonight. There's a bright moon outside. Do you think you can help me?'

"I fought back the tears and nodded.

"My father said, 'Okay, we'll have a bite of supper. . . .'

"We soon finished our bread and milk, but I was still so tired that I could hardly raise my head. As my father went out to feed the pigs, I sat at the table, thinking bitterly, 'I've never smoked or drank; I've always obeyed the Word of Wisdom. The Doctrine and Covenants says that if you obey the Word of Wisdom you will run and not be weary and walk and not faint. And now I'm so tired I can hardly raise my head.' My mouth twitched as I fought to keep back the tears of exhaustion.

"It is impossible to describe what happened, but it seemed as though a beautiful shaft of white light entered my body, filling every fiber of my being. I got up when Father came back, and we went out to the fields.

"My father was a very fast worker, but he couldn't keep up with me that night, even though he worked as fast as he could. I ran for stray bundles, and tossed them, many heavier than I was, from [row to row]. I'll never forget the astonishment in my father's eyes" (Leo W. Spencer, "To Run and Not Be Weary," *Ensign*, Mar. 1974, 45).

### Work

Work is a blessing. It not only enables us to provide for the needs and health of our families, but it also keeps our bodies and minds active and alert. (See 1 Thessalonians 4:11–12 and Psalm 128:2–3.)

### Sufficient Rest

Some people do not sleep long enough to obtain the proper rest. Other people sleep longer than is needed. The Lord has cautioned us to get the sleep we need, but no more than we need. We are all different and must rest according to our needs, but He has told us to go to bed early and to arise early so that both body and mind may be invigorated. (See D&C 88:124.)

### Personal Cleanliness

To prevent sickness, we should bathe, brush our teeth, and wash our hands regularly. We should also regularly wash our clothes, bedding, and dishes.

Sickness and disease can be prevented by eliminating germs. We can eliminate germs by keeping insects and animals out of the home and

*24-b, Exercise is an excellent family project.*

by disposing of animal and human waste. For the same reason, food should be stored in a clean, safe place.

### Proper Diet

A proper diet consists of a variety of foods from each of the food groups every day. We need meats and animal products, fruits and vegetables, dairy products, and grains and starchy roots. (For more information see *The Latter-day Saint Woman: Basic Manual for Women, Part A,* lesson 22: "Nutrition for the Family.")

### Medical and Dental Care

We can protect ourselves and our families from some diseases by getting immunizations and having regular medical checkups. In most parts of the world, immunizations are given by health clinics or physicians. We should also have a dentist check our teeth regularly.

### Physical Exercise and Recreation

- Show visuals 24-a, "Regular physical exercise is necessary for good health," and 24-b, "Exercise is an excellent family project."

In addition to a proper diet, regular physical exercise is necessary for a healthy body. Exercise is something that can be enjoyed both individually and as a family. One benefit of an exercise program for recreation is the opportunity it provides us to be with our families. Each family member will not only be better motivated to exercise, but will also feel closer to the other members of the family.

One excellent exercise almost everyone can do is running. We can run nearly anywhere, at almost any time. Running in place and walking are also good exercises. Basketball, soccer, handball, swimming, bicycling, and other sports can provide both exercise and recreation.

Before beginning any vigorous exercise program, we should get a physical examination. Obtaining and following a doctor's advice about our exercise program will prevent us from doing things that would harm us instead of help us.

### Conclusion

Balance is essential to a healthy life. This means we must strive to achieve balance in work, rest, and recreation. President Brigham Young counseled:

"Let us seek to extend the present life to the uttermost, by observing every law of health, and by properly balancing labor, study, rest, and recreation . . . prepare for a better life. Let us teach these principles to our children, that . . . they may be taught to lay the foundation of health and strength" (*Discourses of Brigham Young* [1954], 186).

The Church needs priesthood holders who have prepared themselves spiritually, intellectually, and physically. Good health helps us be effective in our many responsibilities.

**Challenges**

Survey your personal health problems.

Develop a personal and family physical fitness program.

**Additional Scriptures**

- Proverbs 23:19–23 (we should be wise in choosing what we drink and eat)

- Proverbs 31:1–4 (we should not defile ourselves with strong drink and immorality)

**Teacher Preparation**

Before presenting this lesson:

1. Read *Gospel Principles* chapters 27, "Work and Personal Responsibility," and 29, "The Lord's Law of Health."

2. Assign a class member to give a five-minute report on the contents of the Word of Wisdom (D&C 89:1–17).

3. Assign class members to present any stories, scriptures, or quotations you wish.

# SERVING THE COMMUNITY AND THE NATION

*Lesson 25*

---

The purpose of this lesson is to help us understand our responsibilities to our community and nation.

### Introduction

As members of the Church of Jesus Christ, we should feel a brotherhood and love for all people in all nations of the world, and especially for those in our own neighborhood, community, and nation. We should be loyal to our own country and people and do all we can to help our government meet the needs of the people.

"We believe that governments were instituted of God for the benefit of man," proclaims the Doctrine and Covenants, "and that he holds men accountable for their acts in relation to them" (D&C 134:1).

### Our Individual Responsibilities

Many of society's problems come because some individuals and families do not live honest and moral lives, or do not work to support themselves. Before we can be of service to our community or nation, we must live honest and good lives ourselves. We must first take care of ourselves and our own families and try to overcome any problems that affect us.

Our greatest responsibility is to live the gospel, which will help both ourselves and others. The example of our lives can influence others more than anything we might say. In the Book of Mormon, for example, the people of a wicked city were told that the Lord had spared them only because of the prayers of the righteous who were in the land.

- Ask a class member to read Alma 10:22–23.

The Lord will sometimes bless an entire community because of the righteousness of a few people. Elder David O. McKay spoke of the need for members of the Church to set good examples: "All should take pride in making 'Mormonism' a synonym for trustworthiness, temperance, chastity, honesty, justice—these are fundamental principles of the Church of Jesus Christ of Latter-day Saints, and by exemplifying them in our lives we contribute to the transformation of society, we translate our religion into better social conditions and bring salvation and peace to men here and now" (in Conference Report, Oct. 1927, 14).

We can give great strength to our community and country by living honest and good lives, taking care of our own families, and praying for strength to be proper examples.

## Our Neighborhood and Community Responsibilities

- Show visual 25-a, "Our responsibility to God includes service to others."

Our community has a great need for dependable and honest citizens who are willing to help. The Lord expects us to love and serve our neighbors and friends. This does not require great acts of sacrifice; friendship is often based on small acts of kindness. Part of being a good neighbor is watching out for the needs of others, including widows and orphans. The greatest service we can perform for our neighbors is to introduce the gospel to them. But no matter how they react, we should love them and serve them.

- Ask a class member to read Doctrine and Covenants 58:27–28. Consider for a moment some of the problems facing the people in our community. What are some of the "good causes" we could support in our city or town?

### Education

In some places, schools need to be built or expanded. In other places, schools need better textbooks, teaching aids, and courses of study. The following story tells how some Latter-day Saints improved the quality of education offered at their children's schools:

"One of the features of our favorite city, Seattle, Washington, was the excellent neighborhood public school system. During the twenty years we lived there, we were occasionally tempted to move to the suburbs but always finally decided to stay in the city, partly because of our high regard for the educational opportunities afforded our three children in the public schools. . . .

"In the more recent years, however, we saw a changing school administration begin to depart from the former sound and tested fiscal and educational policies. . . . They began to make radical changes in methods and curriculum. . . . Other policies ruined student morale, fostering serious problems of security, morality, and drug abuse.

"This alarming deterioration motivated many of us to increase our activity and service in the Parent Teacher Association and the elected

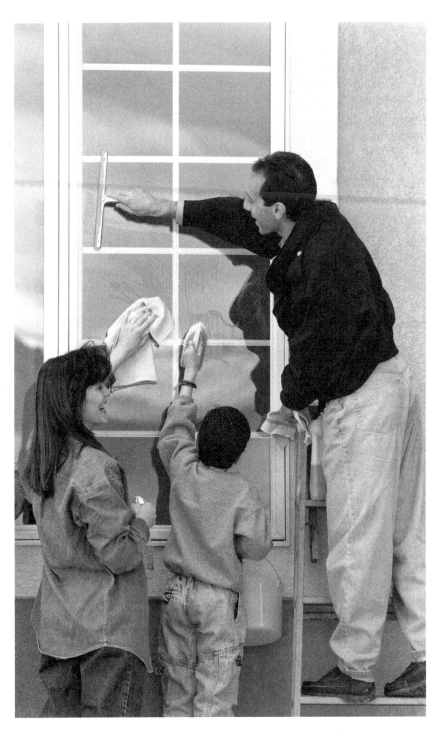

*25-a, Our responsibility to God includes service to others.*

school advisory councils. In a large high school area, roughly corre-
sponding to our ward boundaries, concerned parents and friends
[elected] some of us to positions in both organizations.

"With a Church background for getting things done cooperatively in
meetings, the LDS members began to exert influence upon the school
administration. While supportive of the good programs, we were able
to win an optional return to the traditional curriculum and teaching
methods. To reduce student intimidation and manhandling assaults in
halls and schoolgrounds, and to cut down drug and morality abuses,
we obtained increased security. We won greater parent interest and
involvement and added [the students to our organization]. . . . [We]
proved to the citizens that they had an actual voice in the decisions of
their elected officials. . . .

"These experiences again proved that Latter-day Saints, when they are
cooperatively united and when they actually assert themselves, provide power to leaven a great populace.

"This testimony has led me toward other areas of community, business,
political, and constitutional [involvement]. It has convinced me that
Latter-day Saints not only must, but *can* help produce the social
changes we so desperately need" (David L. Tomlinson, "We Changed
Our Children's Schools," *Ensign,* June 1976, 52–53).

- What educational needs does our community have? What can we as
  individuals and as a priesthood group do to help?

### Morals

We have a responsibility to build communities with high standards
and morals. If our communities are experiencing a decline in moral
values, we can work together to solve these problems. Often, moral
evils can be stopped only if a group of people act together.

- What are the moral problems in our community? What can we do to
  help overcome these problems?

### Health and Safety

Most communities could improve their health and safety conditions.
Some cities need better traffic control or better safety regulations.
Other places need better water or sanitary facilities.

In trying to serve our community, we must consider our community's
own special health and safety needs. Once we have decided which
problems are the most urgent, we can then select one need and make a
plan to help solve it. Members of the Church have been helpful in many
community health and safety projects. Some Church members, for

example, hold political offices, serve on committees, or do volunteer work to improve their communities.

Ted Brewerton, a priesthood holder in Calgary, Canada, is an example of what one person can do to improve his community. He was honored as the most outstanding pharmacist in his province for his work against drug abuse. He distributed pamphlets, gave lectures, visited schools, and helped government officials control the use of drugs. He truly made a difference in the lives of hundreds of people. (See Janice Smith, "Making a Difference," *Ensign*, June 1976, 50.)

Some Latter-day Saints have excused themselves from devoting time to their communities by arguing that they couldn't make a difference for good in society, or that they were too busy. We can all make a difference if we get involved and do something to improve community life.

▪ Discuss the health and safety needs in our area. What can we as priesthood holders do to meet these needs?

*Welfare Service*

It is especially important that Latter-day Saints be willing to help others in times of emergency. A good example of such service occurred in 1976, when a dam broke and flooded several towns near Rexburg, Idaho. Members of the Church from all the surrounding states decided that they would help clean up the towns that had been destroyed or damaged. Young people and priesthood quorums rented buses and traveled to the flooded area. They helped clean out, repair, and build new homes. Several men and women tended children so that the parents could work on their own damaged homes. In a few weeks, most of the cleanup work was done, thanks to the volunteer work of Church members who wanted to serve their fellowmen.

**Responsibilities to Our Country**

President N. Eldon Tanner said, "We would expect every man to be loyal to his native land—the land in which he was born, the land in which he lives, works, and rears his family" (in Conference Report, Apr. 1976, 73; or *Ensign*, May 1976, 48). We need to feel a love for our country and its people and want the best for them. Such love comes naturally as we learn to appreciate the history and sacrifices of those who helped build and strengthen our country.

Being loyal to our country does not mean that we must agree with all of the individuals who lead the government. Most government officials, however, sincerely try to do what is right, and we should give them our support. We should pray daily that they will make proper decisions and do the right things. President Harold B. Lee once had a meeting with the President of the United States in which he "assured him that no matter what his name or his political party, we [the Church] were frequently on our knees, praying God that he and the leaders of this nation and of the world would bring us through the [problems of our times]" (in Conference Report, Apr. 1972, 120; or *Ensign,* July 1972, 29).

Serving our nation also includes obeying its laws. Peace can exist only when everyone obeys the law. The twelfth article of faith states, "We believe in being subject to kings, presidents, rulers, and magistrates, in obeying, honoring, and sustaining the law."

▪ Discuss ways we can show respect for those in authority and obedience to the law. How can we help young men prepare themselves to serve their community and country?

Each country has a different way of making laws. Some countries allow citizens to vote for representatives who help make the laws. Especially in these countries, Latter-day Saints have a duty to be informed about matters of public interest and to support good people as candidates for office. In countries where public elections are held, every citizen should vote.

Some ways we can fulfill our duty to our country are:

1. Be loyal to our country and our people.

2. Pray for our leaders.

3. Obey the law.

4. Be informed about public issues.

5. Support honest and wise leaders.

### Conclusion

As Latter-day Saints we have a responsibility to our community and to our country. We have a duty to live righteously and to help solve the problems and meet the needs of our entire society.

### Challenges

Select one way you can help your neighborhood or community. Make an individual plan and begin to carry it out this week.

With your quorum, decide what your priesthood group might do to improve your community.

In your family prayers, pray for the leaders of the community and nation to lead you in righteousness.

## Additional Scriptures

- 1 Timothy 1:8–10 (the need for law)

- 1 Timothy 2:1–2 (we should pray for government leaders)

- Titus 3:1 (we should obey our governments)

- 1 Peter 2:13–14 (we should submit to the laws established by our governments)

- Mosiah 29 (King Mosiah's discourse on government)

- Doctrine and Covenants 134 (discourse on the need for law and the principles of government)

## Teacher Preparation

Before presenting this lesson:

1. Find out what good causes in your neighborhood and community could use the support of your quorum.

2. Assign class members to present any stories, scriptures, or quotations you wish.

# GOSPEL PRINCIPLES
# AND DOCTRINES

# A TESTIMONY OF THE GOSPEL OF JESUS CHRIST

*Lesson 26*

---

The purpose of this lesson is to help us understand how to obtain and build a strong testimony of the gospel of Jesus Christ.

**Introduction**

Open the meeting by having class members sing "I Know That My Redeemer Lives" (*Hymns,* no. 136; or *Gospel Principles,* 346).

A testimony of the gospel of Jesus Christ is one of the most valuable possessions we can have. President David O. McKay realized this in his youth. He said: "I hungered for it; I felt that if I could get that [a testimony], all else would indeed seem insignificant" ("A Personal Testimony," *Improvement Era,* Sept. 1962, 628).

Our testimonies will sustain us throughout our lives when difficulties and trials come. At such times, we cannot be sustained by the testimonies of others, but will have to rely on our own testimonies in order to endure our trials in faith.

**What Is a Testimony?**

Perhaps we can recall meeting the missionaries for the first time and learning the gospel, or associating with a person who helped us gain a testimony. Or maybe we remember the warm feeling we had when we heard someone bear testimony to us. This feeling is the Holy Ghost bearing witness to our souls that what we are hearing is true. It is a feeling of calm, unwavering certainty. By this feeling, we know that Jesus Christ is the Son of God, that Joseph Smith was a prophet, and that The Church of Jesus Christ of Latter-day Saints is the only true church on the earth. This feeling can also give us a testimony of the Word of Wisdom, of the principle of tithing, or of the truthfulness of the Book of Mormon.

As members of the Church in these latter days, it is also essential that we have a testimony of living prophets. President Harold B. Lee explained the importance of this knowledge:

"I want to impress this upon you. Someone has said it this way, and I believe it to be absolutely true: 'That person is not truly converted until he sees the power of God resting upon the leaders of this church, and until it goes down into his heart like fire.' Until the members of this church have that conviction that they are being led in the right way, and they have a conviction that these men of God are men who are inspired and have been properly appointed by the hand of God, they are not truly converted" (in Conference Report, Apr. 1972, 118; or *Ensign,* July 1972, 103).

- Have the class members think for a moment about their testimonies. Ask them to remember when the truth of the gospel was revealed to them and how they received a spiritual witness that the Church is true, that Jesus is the Christ, or that the Book of Mormon is true. Invite them to share what these experiences were like and how they recognized that they had received a testimony.

### Receiving a Testimony

A testimony is based on revelation from the Holy Ghost. It comes when the Spirit of the Lord speaks to our heart, mind, and spirit and confirms truth to us (see D&C 8:2–3). Christ explained to Peter that his testimony did not come from any human source, but from God (see Matthew 16:13–17).

Elder Parley P. Pratt wrote the following account of the testimony he received that the Book of Mormon was true:

"I opened [the Book of Mormon] with eagerness and read its title page. I then read the testimony of several witnesses in relation to the manner of its being found and translated. . . . I read all day; eating was a burden, I had no desire for food; sleep was a burden when the night came, for I preferred reading to sleep.

"As I read, the spirit of the Lord was upon me, and I knew and comprehended that the book was true, as plainly and manifestly as a man comprehends and knows that he exists. My joy was now full, as it were, and I rejoiced sufficiently to more than pay me for all the sorrows, sacrifices and toils of my life" (*Autobiography of Parley P. Pratt* [1938], 37).

For some, receiving a testimony is a very vivid experience. For others, it is less spectacular, but it is no less important or valuable. Elder Loren C. Dunn said, "It may not come like a flash of light (I don't know how the Lord is going to communicate with you), more than likely it will be the reassurance and a feeling in your heart, a reaffirmation that will come in a rather calm, natural but real way from day to day until you come to a realization that you *do* know" ("Watch Therefore:

For Ye Know Not What Hour," University of Utah Institute devotional, 10 Nov. 1972, 5).

President Marion G. Romney explained that this is the way he received his testimony:

"Sometimes a testimony comes to a person slowly, over an extended period of time. I do not remember a testimony coming to me suddenly. . . . I cannot remember when I did not have a testimony. It has, of course, been strengthened through the years, but I can never remember when I did not believe. But whether a testimony comes suddenly or by degrees, it does something to a person. One is different after he receives a testimony" ("How to Gain a Testimony," *New Era,* May 1976, 11).

There are several things we must do in order to receive a testimony. The five steps that follow are especially important.

- Display a poster of the following five steps, or write the information on the chalkboard:

1. *Desire to Believe.* Alma explains that the first step in gaining a knowledge of the truth is to desire to believe (see Alma 32:26–27).

2. *Search the Scriptures.* Elder Gordon B. Hinckley taught: "I promise you that if you will read the words of that writing which we call scripture, there will come into your heart an understanding and a warmth that will be pleasing to experience. . . . Read, for instance, the Gospel of John from its beginning to its end. Let the Lord speak for himself to you, and his words will come with a quiet conviction that will make the words of his critics meaningless. Read also the testament of the New World, the Book of Mormon, brought forth as a witness 'that Jesus is the Christ, the Eternal God' "("The Miracle That Is Jesus," *Improvement Era,* June 1966, 531).

3. *Do the Will of God.* The Savior makes it clear that a man can know if a doctrine is from God by living the doctrine (see John 7:16–18).

4. *Ponder the Principles of the Gospel.* Pondering the principles of the gospel means studying and thinking about them, then praying with faith in Christ to receive knowledge from the Holy Ghost about what we have learned. (See Moroni 10:3–5.)

5. *Fast and Pray Often.* The prophet Alma came to know for himself that the gospel was true because he fasted and prayed many days. After his fast, the Holy Spirit bore witness of the doctrines of God to his soul. (See Alma 5:45–46.)

- Have the previously assigned class member tell of his experience in gaining a testimony.

**Building a Stronger Testimony**

Once we obtain a testimony, we must continue to strengthen it. President Harold B. Lee said: "Testimony isn't something you have today, and you are going to have always. A testimony is fragile. It is as hard to hold as a moonbeam. It is something you have to recapture every day of your life" ("President Harold B. Lee Directs Church; Led By The Spirit," *Church News*, 15 July 1972, 4).

To strengthen our testimonies each day and to remain happy in the gospel, we must strive to live righteously, perform our priesthood duties, and serve others. A testimony must be a principle of action if it is to increase in strength.

- Show visual 26-a, "We can strengthen our testimonies by bearing them to others."

Sharing our testimonies with others not only strengthens our own testimonies, but also strengthens the testimonies of those who hear us. We are given an opportunity to express our testimonies once a month at our fast and testimony meeting, but we should take advantage of every opportunity to bear our testimonies to our friends and family.

We must be valiant in our testimony of Jesus (see D&C 76:79). As members of the Church, we have the responsibility to share our testimony with others, both members and nonmembers. We demonstrate our testimony each day by what we say and what we do. Peter advised: "Be ready always to give an answer to every man that asketh you a reason of the hope that is in you" (1 Peter 3:15). Our testimonies expose others to the truth and help them desire to know more.

- Have class members read Doctrine and Covenants 62:3 and 84:61. What did the Lord promise to those who bear their testimony?

**Conclusion**

Our testimonies can be a source of strength to our families. A father who was serving a mission in 1868 wrote to his son, "Oh, my son, may your father's testimony be to you a guiding star through all your life" (quoted in Reinhard Maeser, *Karl G. Maeser* [1928], 57).

- Ask the class members how their fathers' testimonies can be "guiding stars" for their lives. Ask the fathers how expressing their testimonies can help their children to gain testimonies.

**Challenges**

Seek to obtain, strengthen, and bear your testimony of the gospel of Jesus Christ.

*26-a, We can strengthen our testimonies by bearing them to others.*

Strive to live worthy of an increasing witness of the truth by living close to the Lord and serving faithfully in your priesthood calling.

Plan a family home evening on the subject of testimony. At the meeting, bear your testimony to your family.

Bear your testimony in fast and testimony meeting.

## Additional Scriptures

- Psalm 19:7 (the value of testimony)

- 1 Corinthians 12:3 (testimonies come from the Holy Ghost)

- 2 Timothy 1:8 (we should not be ashamed to testify)

- Doctrine and Covenants 76:22–23 (the testimony of Joseph Smith and Sidney Rigdon)

## Teacher Preparation

Before presenting this lesson:

1. Prepare the poster suggested in the lesson, or write the information on the chalkboard.

2. Assign a class member to tell of his experience in gaining a testimony.

3. Assign class members to present any stories, scriptures, or quotations you wish.

# FAITH IN JESUS CHRIST

*Lesson 27*

---

The purpose of this lesson is to help us strengthen our faith in Jesus Christ.

### Introduction

Show visual 27-a, "Faith in Jesus Christ is the first principle of the gospel."

Faith in the Lord Jesus Christ is the first principle of the gospel. If we have faith in Jesus Christ, we have confidence in Him; we trust Him and accept Him and His teachings. The Apostle Paul wrote that "we walk by faith, not by sight" (2 Corinthians 5:7). Faith is spiritual proof that things we cannot see or hear do exist and are true. For example, we did not see Jesus die for us or suffer for our sins, but we know through faith that He did. Alma said, "Faith is not to have a perfect knowledge of things; therefore if ye have faith ye hope for things which are not seen, which are true" (Alma 32:21).

### Faith in Jesus Christ

Having faith in Jesus Christ enables us to make sacrifices or to do difficult tasks. Because of their faith, for example, Abraham was willing to offer his son as a sacrifice, Enoch was translated, and Noah was saved from the flood (see Hebrews 11). These and many other miracles were accomplished by faith in Jesus Christ, "for it is by faith that miracles are wrought" (Moroni 7:37).

Faith also enables us to endure suffering, trials, and afflictions. Job was able to endure his great sufferings, for example, because he had faith in Christ. The Lord strengthened Job because the Lord knows and helps those who trust Him. (See Nahum 1:7.)

Although Job suffered more than most of us will ever suffer, he never denied his testimony or turned against God. His children were all killed when his house was destroyed by a great wind. His body was covered with boils. His friends and even his wife mocked him, telling him that he was suffering because he was wicked. But because of his

*27-a, Faith in Jesus Christ is the first principle of the gospel.*

faith, Job endured his trials. At the height of his suffering, he was able to praise God and testify:

"I know that my redeemer liveth, and that he shall stand at the latter day upon the earth:

"And though after my skin worms destroy this body, yet in my flesh shall I see God" (Job 19:25–26). His faith was finally rewarded: his sufferings ended and he was blessed abundantly by the Lord.

The story of Job shows how faith, like an anchor, can help us hold steadfastly to our testimonies when trials come (see Ether 12:4). We may suffer from sickness, poverty, death, or temptation, but as we exercise faith in Jesus Christ, we will be strengthened and blessed.

- What are some other examples from the scriptures about the power of faith? How have you been blessed by your faith in Jesus Christ?

### Strengthening Our Faith in Christ

We should always seek to strengthen our faith. As we do so, we will receive the joy of being close to the Lord and receiving His blessings. Alma tells us that developing faith in Christ is like planting, cultivating, and harvesting the fruit of a tree.

- Show visual 27-b, "Faith begins with the planting of a single seed."

The first step in developing faith can be compared to planting a seed. Alma said, "Experiment upon my words, and exercise a particle of faith, yea, even if ye can no more than desire to believe, let this desire work in you . . . that a seed may be planted" (Alma 32:27–28).

- How can we plant a seed of faith in our hearts?

One of the ways faith begins is when we hear or read the word of God and desire to believe. As we experiment with what we have heard or read, making an effort to believe and to live the principles we have been taught, we begin to feel in our hearts that what we have been taught is true. (See John 7:16–17.)

- Show visual 27-c, "Just as a plant needs sunlight, air, and water, faith needs constant nourishment."

The second step is similar to caring for a plant. Just as a plant needs sunlight, air, and water to grow, our faith needs nourishment if it is to grow.

- How can we nourish or increase our faith in Jesus Christ?

We can nourish our faith by reading and pondering the scriptures, fasting and praying, serving the Lord, sustaining our Church leaders, and

*27-b, Faith begins with the planting of a single seed.*

*27-c, Just as a plant needs sunlight, air, and water,
faith needs constant nourishment.*

obeying God's commandments. Just as a plant without water will die, faith without action will die. We must constantly nourish our faith through righteous works. (See James 2:14–26.)

- Show visual 27-d, "The harvest of faith is peace and joy and eternal life."

Through our diligence in nourishing our faith, we will be able to enjoy great blessings, just as caring for a plant will allow us to enjoy its fruit.

- What are the blessings, or fruits, of faith in Jesus Christ?

Faith enables us to:

"Cleave unto every good thing" (see Moroni 7:28).

Enjoy peace and happiness without fearing the future.

Receive answers to our prayers.

Have our burdens lightened by God (see Matthew 11:28–29).

Be forgiven of our sins as we repent of them.

Exercise the power of the priesthood.

Have the Holy Ghost with us (see Moroni 7:32).

Experience miracles in our lives (see 2 Nephi 26:13).

Return to live with our Heavenly Father after the Resurrection.

The Bible tells of a woman who had been very ill for 12 years. She had spent all she had trying to be cured by the doctors, but they were unable to cure her. One day Jesus came to her village. She had heard of Jesus and had faith that she would be healed even if she could only touch His robe. And so, exercising her faith, she touched the Savior as He walked by her. Upon touching His robe, she was immediately healed, and Jesus turned to her and said, "Daughter, be of good comfort: thy faith hath made thee whole." (See Luke 8:43–48.)

The woman in this story nourished her faith in Christ by putting her belief into action. She touched the Savior's robe and thus received the blessings of her faith by being cured.

- Why is it important to exercise faith in Jesus Christ when blessing the sick and when being blessed?

- Share the following story:

Randall Ellsworth was a missionary who exercised great faith after being seriously hurt by an earthquake in Guatemala. At the time of the earthquake, he was in a building and the building collapsed on him. A General Authority described his experience this way:

*27-d, The harvest of faith is peace and joy and eternal life.*

"[He was] pinned for, I think, twelve hours. Found himself totally paralyzed from the waist down. Kidney functions, not present. No hope to ever walk again. . . .

"He was flown to . . . Maryland and . . . interviewed in the hospital by a television reporter. The television reporter said to him, 'The doctors say you will not walk again. What do you think, Elder Ellsworth?' He said, 'I'll not only walk again, but I have a call from a prophet to serve a mission in Guatemala, and I shall go back to Guatemala and finish that mission. . . .'

"He exercised [two times the amount] outlined by the doctors. He exerted his faith. He received a blessing from the priesthood and his recovery was miraculous. It astounded the physicians and the specialists. He began to be able to stand on his feet. Then he could walk with crutches, and then the doctors said to him, 'You may return to the mission field if the Church will permit you to go.' He went. We sent him to Guatemala. He returned to the land to which he had been called, to the people whom he dearly loved.

"While there he was walking, proselyting a full schedule with a cane in each hand. [One day his mission president] looked at him and said, 'Elder Ellsworth, with the faith that you have, why don't you throw those canes away and walk?' . . . He put down the canes and has never used them since" (Thomas S. Monson, quoted by Marion G. Romney, in Conference Report, Oct. 1977, 61–62; or *Ensign,* Nov. 1977, 42).

- Have a previously assigned quorum member describe a time in his life when he had to live by faith during a personal crisis or trial.

### Conclusion

In order for our faith to grow, we must nourish it constantly. It is a gift and blessing that we need at all times and in all places. Everything we do in the Church requires faith in Jesus Christ. For example, paying tithing, serving in the Church, or saving enough money to go to the temple all require faith. As we nourish our faith in Jesus Christ by obeying Him, studying His gospel, praying, fasting, attending our meetings, and serving in the Church, we will receive many wonderful blessings. The greatest blessing of developing our faith is that we, along with our families, can be worthy to return to our Father in Heaven.

### Challenges

Exercise your faith in Jesus Christ when you are called to perform a priesthood ordinance, such as administering to the sick.

Apply the principle of faith in meeting personal problems.

## Additional Scriptures

- Mark 6:5–6 (miracles cannot be performed in the absence of faith)

- Hebrews 11 (discourse on the power of faith)

- 1 Peter 1:3–9 (salvation comes through faith)

- Enos 1:4–8, 15 (sin is forgiven through faith)

- Ether 12:12–21 (examples of the power of faith)

## Teacher Preparation

Before presenting this lesson:

1. Read *Gospel Principles* chapter 18, "Faith in Jesus Christ."

2. Study Hebrews, chapter 11.

3. Assign a class member to describe a time in his life when he had to live by faith during a personal crisis or trial.

4. Assign class members to present any stories, scriptures, or quotations you wish.

# REPENTANCE

*Lesson 28*

The purpose of this lesson is to help us understand how repentance can prepare us to return to our Heavenly Father.

## Introduction

The Prophet Joseph Smith gave this challenge: "Let us this very day begin anew, and now say, with all our hearts, we will forsake our sins and be righteous" (*Teachings of the Prophet Joseph Smith*, sel. Joseph Fielding Smith [1976], 364).

Because all of us are on the earth to learn and to grow, we all make mistakes. There are many kinds of mistakes. Sometimes we do things we know we should not do, such as being unkind or taking something that does not belong to us. Sometimes we fail to do the things we know we should do, such as paying our tithing or being good home teachers.

## The Need for Repentance

When we know we have done wrong, we cannot be happy. We feel ashamed of our mistakes and find we cannot serve the Lord properly. Sometimes, our unhappiness may even cause us to treat others unkindly. Our Heavenly Father does not want us to be unhappy. He wants all of us to receive the blessings He has for us, but He will not give us blessings we don't deserve. This does not mean that He has turned away or loves us less. It simply means that He wants us to overcome our weaknesses. Repentance can help us overcome our weaknesses and thereby become worthy to live with our Heavenly Father.

For this reason we need to examine our lives to discover where we need to improve. President Joseph Fielding Smith taught: "It is our duty to be better today than we were yesterday, and better tomorrow than we are today. Why? Because we are on that road . . . to perfection, and that can only come through obedience and the desire in our hearts to overcome [our sins]" (*Doctrines of Salvation*, comp. Bruce R. McConkie, 3 vols. [1954–56], 2:18–19).

- Read Alma 11:37. Why is repentance necessary? Read 1 John 1:8–10, Alma 34:33–34, and 3 Nephi 30. Why should we repent as soon as possible?

## How Does a Person Repent?

Sin is like dirt on our bodies. It makes us spiritually unclean. Repentance is like washing off the dirt. After repenting, we feel refreshed and clean. Elder A. Theodore Tuttle explained it this way:

"Repentance is like soap. It is the soap of life. Like soap, it washes away the sins of life. It is to be used as frequently as necessary. One must keep in mind, however, that misuse—lack of thorough cleansing and half-hearted effort—may result in 'tattletale gray.' Properly used, however, the soap of life cleanses thoroughly, completely, and permanently. . . .

"One day we . . . will be ushered before the judgment bar of the Lord. There we shall stand either besmirched, dirty, and unclean, or by acceptance and application of the great and marvelous gift of cleansing—by the soap of life—we may stand clean, forgiven, and pure before the Lord. The next time you use soap, you might also want to think of cleansing your spirit by applying the soap of life, the universal law of repentance" ("Repentance," *Improvement Era,* Nov. 1968, 64, 67).

In order to repent, we must follow certain steps.

- Discuss the seven parts of repentance as explained in the *Gospel Principles* manual, chapter 19. If possible, let several brethren each take one part, prepare to discuss it, and then present it to the class. Display a poster which lists the seven parts of repentance while they are being discussed, or refer to them on the chalkboard. (The seven parts are recognizing sin, feeling sorrow for sin, forsaking sin, confessing sin, making restitution, forgiving others, and keeping the commandments of God.)

- Display visual 28-a, "True repentance takes time and effort."

True repentance is not easy. It takes time and effort. For this reason, we cannot put off the day of our repentance (see Alma 13:27).

## The Joy of Repentance

- Show visual 28-b, "Repentance is possible because Jesus Christ has paid for our sins."

We repent to gain forgiveness of our sins. But if Jesus Christ had not paid for our sins and died for us, we could never be forgiven. It is only through His atoning sacrifice that mercy can satisfy justice and we can have our sins cleansed from us (see Alma 34:10–16). This is a great blessing, and we should always be thankful for it.

*28-a, True repentance takes time and effort.*

Jesus paid for our sins, but they are not removed from us unless we repent. When Alma was describing how he recognized and repented of his sins, he said:

"I did remember all my sins and iniquities, for which I was tormented with the pains of hell. . . .

". . . I remembered also to have heard my father prophesy unto the people concerning the coming of one Jesus Christ, a Son of God, to atone for the sins of the world.

"Now, as my mind caught hold upon this thought, I cried within my heart: O Jesus, thou Son of God, have mercy on me. . . .

"And now, behold, when I thought this, I could remember my pains no more. . . .

"And oh, what joy, and what marvelous light I did behold; yea, my soul was filled with joy as exceeding as was my pain" (Alma 36:13, 17–20).

▪ Briefly review the parable of the prodigal son (see Luke 15:11–32). What did the prodigal son feel as he began the process of repentance? What did his father feel?

The story of the prodigal son is often repeated in modern life, as in the following story:

▪ Share the following story of a modern prodigal son. Have the class members silently identify the steps of repentance as the story is told.

"Until I was 17 years of age, I stayed close to the Church, attending all my meetings and carrying out my priesthood responsibilities. It did not occur to me to do otherwise. I loved the Church and its programs.

"At 17, however, I began to 'flex my teenage muscles,' rebelling against family direction and demanding my 'free agency.' One of my best friends was of another faith, and I fell into the trap of trying some of the things he offered—alcohol, tobacco. I dated non-LDS girls and soon fell in love with a wonderful young lady. Her parents invited me to their summer cabin on many weekends, and this, of course, kept me from church activity.

"Then World War II came along, and when my bishop asked me if I wanted to go on a mission, I said I would rather join the military and serve my country. I still believe serving one's country is important, but I know now that I would have been wiser to serve a mission for my Heavenly Father first.

"Also, about this time, I began finding out that some Church members whom I admired greatly were not observing all the standards of the Church. I let myself become their judge, and to me they were hypocrites.

*28-b, Repentance is possible because Jesus Christ has paid for our sins.*

I covenanted with myself that if I ever failed to live our standards, rather than be a hypocrite by teaching one thing and doing another, I would stay away from the Church. This was another serious error, for this is just what I did and just what the adversary wanted.

"Four years as a Navy pilot and 15 years of traveling in the sales profession made it easy for me to remain inactive, yet all during these years I believed the truths that were deeply implanted in my soul. When I was 38, my youngest brother, Tom, moved in with us for six weeks. Each Sunday morning he went alone to his priesthood and other meetings, and my conscience began to prick me. I wasn't happy, I knew something was wrong, and this feeling kept coming back with greater frequency. In the past I had been able to give up smoking whenever I wanted, but now I found I could not. I would visit Tom in his office and find myself striking out at the Church in criticism, and afterwards, although I would never tell him so, I felt guilty.

"I was building up to my hour of crisis, and it came one night after a cocktail party and dance at the country club. I retired to my bed late but could not sleep, almost unheard of for me. Finally I arose so as not to disturb my lovely wife, and for the first time in my life I paced the floor, finally realizing I had to change.

"I had never been able to show emotion through tears and humility, but the next thing I remember I was on my knees pleading with my Heavenly Father for help for the first time in 19 years. As I prayed, an overwhelming feeling of love and compassion and happiness filled my being, and the Holy Ghost encompassed me with such power that I sobbed convulsively for a considerable time. When I arose, I felt good. Gratitude and thankfulness filled my heart. Never in my life had I known such a feeling of warmth, and an inner burning filled my entire being with such intensity that I thought I was going to be consumed.

"I went to our bedroom and awakened my wife. I was still crying, and she asked me what was wrong. I told her of my desire to change my life and encompass the gospel of Jesus Christ, and she told me instantly that she would support me. From that moment I have never had a desire for a cigarette, a drink of any type, or a cup of coffee.

"The Lord began blessing me, and he has never stopped to this day. Within a year it was my privilege to baptize my children and, soon afterward, my wife. A year later we went to the Logan Temple to be married for eternity and to have our children sealed to us.

"I testify that the Lord is pleased when his lost sheep come home. He shows his love and kindness to all of us when we repent of our sins and keep his commandments" (Lewis W. Cottle, "The Return of the Prodigal," *Ensign,* Mar. 1974, 43–44).

- What were the feelings of this modern prodigal son as he repented? Read Luke 15:10. How does our Heavenly Father view our repentance? (see D&C 58:42 and Isaiah 1:18).

## Conclusion

We all need to repent if we are to become like our Heavenly Father and live with Him again. For this reason Jesus Christ atoned for our sins and made it possible for us to repent. When we do repent of our sins, we bring joy to ourselves and to our Heavenly Father.

President Harold B. Lee taught: "The most important of all the commandments of God is that one that you're having the most difficulty keeping today. If it's one of dishonesty, if it's one of unchastity, if it's one of falsifying, not telling the truth, today is the day for you to work on that until you've been able to conquer that weakness. Then you start on the next one that's most difficult for you to keep" ("Californians Hear President Lee," *Church News*, 5 May 1973, 3).

## Challenges

Plead with the Lord in your personal prayers to help you overcome the problems you are working on. Report to Him each day on your progress, and as you endeavor to improve, continue to pray for forgiveness for past mistakes.

## Additional Scriptures

- Psalm 51:10 (David prays for forgiveness)

- Isaiah 1:16–18 (we are commanded to repent)

- Luke 15:7 (heaven rejoices over those who repent)

- 2 Corinthians 7:10 (godly sorrow brings repentance)

- Mosiah 4:1–3 (sins are forgiven because of Christ's Atonement)

- Alma 7:15 (baptism as a sign of repentance)

- Alma 12:14–15 (faith and repentance bring salvation)

- Alma 34:8–9 (Christ atoned for the sins of the world)

- Doctrine and Covenants 19:16–17 (Christ suffered for those who repent)

- Doctrine and Covenants 76:40–42 (Jesus died to atone for the sins of the world)

**Teacher Preparation**

Before presenting this lesson:

1. Read *Gospel Principles* chapter 19, "Repentance."

2. Prepare the poster suggested in the lesson, or write the information on the chalkboard.

3. Prepare the lesson so as to avoid discussions of quorum members' personal problems.

4. If you desire, assign several class members to discuss the seven steps of repentance identified in chapter 19 of the *Gospel Principles* manual.

5. Assign class members to present any stories, scriptures, or quotations you wish.

# BAPTISM,
# A CONTINUING
# COVENANT

*L e s s o n    2 9*

---

The purpose of this lesson is to encourage us to continue keeping the covenants we made at baptism.

## Introduction

Each of us who has been baptized has done so as a sign that he has changed his life and is willing to obey the principles that lead toward exaltation. But just being baptized is not enough. At that time, we began a new way of life, and to obtain the blessings of that new life, we must continue progressing and improving ourselves.

The prophet Alma, concerned about his priesthood brethren after their baptism, told them: "And now behold, I ask of you, my brethren of the church, have ye spiritually been born of God? Have ye received his image in your countenances? Have ye experienced this mighty change in your hearts?" (Alma 5:14). These questions are just as important today. Have we all felt a change in our hearts and experienced a spiritual rebirth since our baptism into the Church of Jesus Christ?

Many people enjoy a spiritual feeling at the time of their baptism. One member described it this way: "I will never forget the emotion inside my soul; to be clean, to start fresh as a child of God. . . . It was such a special feeling!" (Vivian Ford, "Ask and Ye Shall Receive," *No More Strangers*, 4 vols., ed. Hartman Rector and Connie Rector [1971–90], 3:175). This feeling can continue if we always strive to keep our baptismal covenants.

## Our Baptismal Covenant

- Show visual 29-a, "At baptism we make a covenant with God to keep His commandments."

A covenant is an agreement or promise between two or more people. At baptism we made a very important covenant with God. President Spencer W. Kimball said: "To be baptized is to enter into a covenant [with God] . . . to *do*, not merely to refrain from doing, to work righteousness as well as to avoid evil" (*The Miracle of Forgiveness* [1969], 94).

*29-a, At baptism we make a covenant with God to keep His commandments.*

- Have the class members read and mark Doctrine and Covenants 20:37 and Mosiah 18:8–10. What specific covenants did we make with the Lord when we were baptized? (List the covenants on the chalkboard as shown below.)

We covenanted to:

Enter the Church of Jesus Christ.

Be called after His name.

Serve God and keep His commandments.

Serve each other and bear each other's burdens.

Be a witness for Christ and His Church.

These scriptures also tell us about God's part of the baptismal covenant.

- What did the Lord promise us when we were baptized? (List the responses on the chalkboard. Answers should include those listed below.)

The Lord promised to:

Forgive our sins.

Give us the guidance of the Holy Ghost.

Let us come forth in the first resurrection.

Give us eternal life.

Baptism is the beginning of the "mighty change" we must all experience in order to return to our Father in Heaven (see Alma 5:13–14 and Mosiah 5:7–9). As we live up to our covenants, our desires and actions change and we become more and more like our Father in Heaven. When we are baptized we are placed under the water. The scriptures compare this to burying, or leaving behind, our old self (see Romans 6:4; D&C 76:51). When we come out of the water, we are washed clean of sin and begin a new life. This new life began with a lasting agreement with God; and if we do our part, He will do His. As we obey Him, He will help us change and lead us back into His presence.

- Have two previously assigned brethren describe how they felt when they were baptized and how their lives have changed since baptism. Involve the youth in this part of the lesson.

## Our Progress after Baptism

Some people think that salvation comes simply by being baptized. Baptism, however, is only a beginning. We must continue to grow in righteousness after baptism if we are to achieve eternal life. To help us do this, the Lord has given us certain commandments to keep after baptism.

- Have the class read Moroni 6:4–9. What obligations do we have after baptism? (One answer is following the guidance of the Holy Ghost, but this will be discussed in the next lesson.)

Our responsibilities following baptism include:

Praying.

Fasting.

Attending Church meetings.

Partaking of the sacrament.

Helping others.

Repenting of our sins.

Following the guidance of the Holy Ghost (this will be discussed in the next lesson).

As we go about our duties of making a living, attending school, and doing necessary chores, we often get involved in worldly problems and forget our covenants. The challenge we all face, therefore, is how to keep our spirituality and covenants. The things Moroni mentioned can help us continue in the new life we began at baptism.

### Praying

Sincere personal prayer is important if we are to have the strength we need to live the gospel commandments. Prayer keeps us close to our Father in Heaven and allows us to express our thanks to Him as well as discuss our problems with Him. We should consider it a great blessing to open and close each day of our lives with prayer.

### Fasting

At least once a month, prayer should be combined with fasting. In the Church, we usually fast for two meals on fast Sunday. As individuals, we may fast whenever we need guidance and additional spiritual strength. (See lesson 31 in this manual.)

*29-b, We renew our baptismal covenants when we partake of the sacrament.*

## *Attending Church Meetings*

We can gain spiritual strength by regularly attending Church meetings, where we learn more about the gospel and strengthen our testimonies. We should encourage family members to attend all of their Church meetings. When we attend these meetings, we should participate in them by singing, pondering, giving talks, and being reverent.

## *Partaking of the Sacrament*

- Show visual 29-b, "We renew our baptismal covenants when we partake of the sacrament."

The most important reason to attend sacrament meeting is to take the sacrament. The covenants we make when we partake of the sacrament renew the covenants we made at baptism. In this way, each week during the sacrament we remember our baptismal covenants and promise again that we will keep them.

- Read Doctrine and Covenants 20:77. How are the covenants we make each Sunday similar to our baptismal covenants?

## *Helping Others*

When we were baptized, we promised the Lord that we would be willing to "bear one another's burdens, . . . mourn with those that mourn; yea, and comfort those that stand in need of comfort" (Mosiah 18:8–9). Service to others—helping the needy, teaching our families, being concerned about the welfare of all people—is part of our baptismal covenant with the Lord. It is an important part of the new life we must live after baptism.

## *Repenting of Our Sins*

We all make mistakes, and therefore must repent to keep ourselves clean (see lesson 28 of this manual). Through repentance we can be cleansed again from our sins and thus be worthy to receive the guidance of the Holy Ghost.

## The Way to Perfection

We will always need our baptismal covenants. We must continue perfecting our lives, exchanging bad habits for good ones. President Spencer W. Kimball said: "Certainly self-mastery is a continuous program—a journey, not a single start. Men do not suddenly become righteous any more than a tiny acorn suddenly becomes an oak. Advancement to perfection can nevertheless be rapid if one resolutely strides toward the goal" (*The Miracle of Forgiveness* [1969], 210).

The prophet Nephi taught that after baptism we "must press forward" and "endure to the end." He promised that God will give us eternal life if we show our love by obeying Him (see 2 Nephi 31:19–21). As we obey the Lord and keep the covenants we made with Him at the time of baptism, we will experience happiness in this life and eternal joy in the life to come.

President Joseph Fielding Smith explained our need to endure to the end in keeping our covenants: "One of the great purposes of the true church is to teach men what they must do after baptism to gain the full blessing of the gospel. . . . We must endure to the end; we must keep the commandments after baptism; we must work out our salvation . . . ; we must so live as to acquire the attributes of godliness and become the kind of people who can enjoy the glory and wonders of the celestial kingdom" ("The Plan of Salvation," *Ensign*, Nov. 1971, 5).

**Conclusion**

A member of another faith who later joined the Church explained what her baptism meant to her:

"Everything I saw and heard in the Church impressed me very, very much. The warmth and love, as well as the deep concern each member had for the other members, made me realize that this religion must have something special about it. . . .

"I [soon] realized . . . that I was in the wrong church and that The Church of Jesus Christ of Latter-day Saints is the only true church on this earth. I knew too that I had . . . to join it. . . .

"The transition from the former to the present life was not easy, but the thing that has sustained me throughout the entire experience was and is the renewal of my baptismal covenants each week at sacrament meetings—my covenant to take the Savior's name upon me, to always remember him, and to keep his commandments, and the Lord's covenant in turn that, if I honor these promises, his Spirit will always be with me. . . .

". . . I remember my baptism and the total immersion in the water. To me it symbolizes death to selfishness and sin and rising to newness of life as a child of God. This act of baptism, too, I think, is symbolic of the way Heavenly Father wants us to live—overcoming selfishness and fighting temptation. In this manner we 'die' to self and sin and rise and progress *daily* on the road back into our Father's presence.

"Then I silently renew my covenant to take the name of Jesus Christ upon me, telling him that I renew the promise to accept him, the principles of the gospel, and his teachings; to accept the Church and to uphold the prophet and the other Church authorities, the only ones divinely commissioned to lead us in the name of God. In my silent prayer I add that I renew the covenant to always remember him, for example, to recall his presence, especially during the day in moments of temptation or weariness. Finally I renew the covenant to keep his commandments, knowing that if I do this faithfully I will have his Spirit to be with me" (Miriam Spain Peterson, "The Lord Takes Care," in *No More Strangers,* 4 vols., ed. Hartman Rector and Connie Rector [1971–90], 3:154, 157–59).

### Challenge

Examine the progress of your life since your baptism. At that time you probably felt a "change of heart" begin within you. As the prophet Alma asks, "Can ye feel so now?" (Alma 5:26). Can you still feel the "newness of life" mentioned in the scriptures? If something is lacking, begin today to repent and correct the problem.

### Additional Scriptures

- Galatians 3:27–29 (we take upon us the name of Christ at baptism)

- 1 Peter 3:21 (baptism is a prerequisite of salvation)

- Doctrine and Covenants 27:2 (we partake of the sacrament in remembrance of Christ)

---

### Teacher Preparation

Before presenting this lesson:

1. Read *Gospel Principles* chapter 20, "Baptism."

2. Read lessons 28 and 31 of this manual.

3. Prepare the poster suggested in the lesson, or write the information on the chalkboard.

4. Assign two class members to describe how they felt when they were baptized and how their lives have changed since baptism. Involve the youth in this part of the lesson.

5. Assign class members to present any stories, scriptures, or quotations you wish.

# THE GIFT OF THE HOLY GHOST

*Lesson 30*

---

The purpose of this lesson is to help us understand the great blessings that can come through the gift of the Holy Ghost.

**Introduction**

After we are baptized, we are given the gift of the Holy Ghost by the laying on of hands. Concerning the gift of the Holy Ghost, President Lorenzo Snow counseled: "We should try to learn the nature of this spirit, that we may understand its suggestions, and then we will always be able to do right. . . . From the time we . . . [receive] the gift of the Holy Ghost, we have a friend, if we do not drive it from us by doing wrong. That friend is the Holy Spirit" (in Conference Report, Apr. 1899, 52).

- Show visual 30-a, "The gift of the Holy Ghost is the right to have the Holy Ghost as a constant companion."

- How is the Holy Ghost like a friend?

- Have class members read John 14:16, 17, 26 and 16:13. Why do we need the Holy Ghost to be our companion and friend? (List responses on the chalkboard. Answers may include the following.)

---

Some of the ways the Holy Ghost helps us are:

1. He reveals truth to us.
2. He helps teach us the gospel.
3. He helps us remember things.
4. He comforts us in times of sorrow.
5. He protects us from evil.
6. He inspires us as we teach the gospel in talks and lessons.
7. He warns us when we are in danger.
8. He tells us all things we should do.

---

Elder LeGrand Richards made this statement: "I would rather have my children and my children's children enjoy the companionship of the Holy Ghost than any other companionship in this world because if they will heed the promptings of that Spirit, he will lead them into all truth and see them safely back into the presence of their Father in heaven" (in Conference Report, Apr. 1966, 112; or *Improvement Era,* June 1966, 540).

Because the guidance of the Holy Ghost is so important, we should do all we can to be worthy of His companionship.

### Keeping the Holy Ghost with Us

There are many things we can do to keep the Holy Ghost with us. One way is to partake of the sacrament worthily. Each time we partake of the sacrament, we promise that we will obey the Lord's commandments. If we keep our promise, the Lord has promised us that we can "always have his Spirit" with us. (See D&C 20:77.)

Another way to keep the Holy Ghost with us is to keep our bodies morally clean. The Apostle Paul taught that our bodies are like temples and that we must not defile them (see 1 Corinthians 3:16–17). The Holy Ghost cannot dwell in unclean temples; it is important, therefore, that we keep our bodies clean and pure in thought, speech, dress, and action, avoiding even the appearance of evil. Elder Melvin J. Ballard said, "The Holy Ghost is the most sensitive spirit I know anything about" (quoted in *1967–68 Priesthood Study Course: Deacons Quorum,* 70). Because He is so sensitive, the Holy Ghost can be offended by what we may consider unimportant things.

To keep the Holy Ghost with us, we must live in harmony with those around us. Speaking to the Nephites, Christ said that the spirit of contention comes from the devil (see 3 Nephi 11:29). The Holy Ghost cannot dwell where disunity and disharmony exist. For this reason, arguing with our wife or quarreling with a brother or sister will drive the Holy Ghost away from us and from our homes.

The Prophet Joseph Smith, for example, could not receive any inspiration from the Lord unless he had the right feelings toward everyone. One morning he became upset about something his wife had done. Later, when he tried to translate some of the Book of Mormon, he found he could not. Concerned, he went to an orchard and prayed, and then he came back to the house and asked Emma's forgiveness. Only then was he able to translate. (See B. H. Roberts, *A Comprehensive History of the Church,* 1:131.)

Our need for the Holy Ghost is just as great as the Prophet's was. We need the Holy Ghost to guide us in our responsibilities and especially in directing our families. When our children do wrong, for example,

*30-a, The gift of the Holy Ghost is the right to have the
Holy Ghost as a constant companion.*

we should not lose our tempers but should ask the Holy Ghost to direct us in correcting them (see D&C 121:43).

- What are some things we do that prevent the Holy Ghost from being our companion? What can we do to keep His companionship?

President Joseph Fielding Smith said:

"The Holy Ghost will not dwell with that person who is unwilling to obey and keep the commandments of God. . . . In such a soul the spirit of the Holy Ghost cannot enter.

"That great gift comes to us only through humility and faith and obedience. . . . Did you ever stop to think what a great privilege it is for us to have the companionship of one of the members of the Godhead? Have you thought of it that way? That is our privilege, if we keep the commandments the Lord has given us" ("Fundamental Gospel Truths Balance Education For Students At BYU," *Church News,* 4 Nov. 1961, 14).

**Ways the Holy Ghost Helps Us**

When we show by our faithfulness that we desire to have the Holy Ghost as our companion, He helps us in the following ways to live happier and better lives:

*He Helps Us Be Better People*

The Holy Ghost "inspires virtue, kindness, goodness, tenderness, gentleness, and charity" (Parley P. Pratt, *Key to the Science of Theology,* 4th ed. [1877], 102).

*He Shows Us What to Do*

The Holy Ghost can help us make important decisions.

- Read Doctrine and Covenants 6:15 and 8:2. How does the Holy Ghost help us make decisions?

*He Guides Us As We Serve in the Church*

Elder Franklin D. Richards related how the Holy Ghost guided him: "I have heard the still small voice, or the whisperings of the Spirit, as I have counseled with you, my brothers and sisters; as I have conferred the priesthood upon men; as I have set men and women apart to positions in the Church; as I have given blessings to the sick; as I have borne my testimony to nonmembers as well as members; as I have been delivering a sermon, and at many other times" (in Conference Report, Apr. 1973, 171–72; or *Ensign,* July 1973, 117).

*He Warns Us*

There are times when the Holy Ghost warns us of danger or temptation. Elder Franklin D. Richards told of a young father who "was awakened one night by a voice that clearly told him to get up and go downstairs. He heeded the warning, and in going into the kitchen he found one wall engulfed in flames. Hurriedly he awakened his family and called the fire department, and with the help of his family he fought the fire, keeping it down until the fire department arrived and put it out.

"There was no question in his mind that this warning was a manifestation of the protection the Holy Ghost can give to those who keep their lives in harmony with the Spirit" (in Conference Report, Apr. 1973, 171; or *Ensign,* July 1973, 117).

### He Can Comfort Us

One of the roles of the Holy Ghost is to be a comforter in times of pain or sorrow. At such times, the Holy Ghost can help us find peace and understanding. Elder Franklin D. Richards related the following experience: "It was my privilege to meet two wonderful women, close friends, who had lost their husbands in a tragic airplane accident. Did I find them in despair and deep mourning? No, indeed. I have never witnessed greater courage and strength. They bore witness to the fact that they had truly felt the comfort of the Spirit, . . . that they had an assurance that all would be well with them and their families as they lived close to the Church and kept the commandments of the Lord" (in Conference Report, Apr. 1973, 171; or *Ensign,* July 1973, 117).

▪ Share the following story with class members.

President Heber J. Grant told how the Holy Ghost brought knowledge and comfort to members of his family:

"About one hour before my wife died, I called my children into her room and told them that their mother was dying and for them to bid her good-bye. One of the little girls, about twelve years of age, said to me: 'Papa, I do not want my mamma to die. I have been with you in the hospital . . . for six months; . . . [every time] mamma was in distress you had administered to her and she has been relieved of her pain and quietly gone to sleep. I want you to lay hands upon my mamma and heal her.'

"I told my little girl that we all had to die sometime, and that I felt assured in my heart that her mother's time had arrived. She and the rest of the children left the room.

"I then knelt down by the bed of my wife (who by this time had lost consciousness) and I told the Lord I acknowledged His hand in life, in death, in joy, in sorrow, in prosperity, or adversity. I thanked Him for the knowledge I had that my wife belonged to me for all eternity. . . . But I told the Lord that I lacked the strength to have my wife die and to have it affect the faith of my little children . . . ; and I [asked] the Lord with all the strength that I possessed, that He would give to that little girl of mine a knowledge that it was His mind and His will that her mamma should die.

"Within an hour my wife passed away, and I called the children back into the room. My little boy about five and a half or six years of age was weeping bitterly, and the little girl twelve years of age took him in her arms and said: 'Do not weep, do not cry, Heber; since we went out of this room the voice of the Lord from heaven has said to me, 'In the death of your mamma the will of the Lord shall be done.' . . .

"I . . . know that God hears and answers prayers! [I know] that in the hour of adversity the Latter-day Saints are comforted and blessed and consoled as no other people are!" (*Gospel Standards*, comp. G. Homer Durham [1941], 361).

### He Testifies of the Truth

It is through the Holy Ghost that we receive our testimony of the gospel. In the same way, the Holy Ghost will help us know when our leaders are speaking by the power of the Holy Ghost. President Henry D. Moyle taught: "We can tell when the speakers are moved by the Holy Ghost only when we ourselves are moved upon by the Holy Ghost. Therefore, it is essential that the membership of the Church be just as diligent in their faith as their leaders" ("Revelation: Yesterday and Today," *Improvement Era*, June 1962, 407).

- Invite a previously assigned class member to relate an experience in which he felt the companionship of the Holy Ghost.

### Conclusion

The gift of the Holy Ghost is a great blessing given to those who have been confirmed members of the Church. If we live worthy of His companionship, He will help us to successfully complete our missions here on earth. He will do this by guiding us, protecting us, comforting us, and otherwise helping us in all areas of our lives.

### Challenge

Seek the companionship of the Holy Ghost in your daily life. To know the areas in which you need to improve to have the Holy Ghost as a constant companion, ask yourself the following questions:

1. Am I trying to keep all the commandments?

2. Am I praying regularly?

3. How am I showing my love for the Savior?

4. How am I showing my love for others?

5. Am I keeping my thoughts and actions pure?

6. Do I thank the Lord for His blessings, including the gift of the Holy Ghost?

**Additional Scriptures**

▪ Acts 5:32 (the Holy Ghost comes to the obedient)

▪ 1 Nephi 10:17–19 (power and knowledge from the Holy Ghost come through faith in Christ)

▪ 2 Nephi 31:13 (the Holy Ghost is received following faith, repentance, and baptism)

▪ Moses 6:61 (the powers and blessings of the Holy Ghost)

**Teacher Preparation**

Before presenting this lesson:

1. Read *Gospel Principles* chapter 21, "The Gift of the Holy Ghost."

2. Invite a class member to prepare to relate an experience in which he felt the companionship of the Holy Ghost.

3. Assign class members to present any stories, scriptures, or quotations you wish.

# PRAYER AND FASTING

*Lesson 31*

---

The purpose of this lesson is to help us learn how to strengthen our families and quorums through prayer and fasting.

### Introduction

- Have the assigned class members present a short review of the principles of fasting and prayer as taught in the *Gospel Principles* manual.

### Praying and Fasting Can Be a Blessing to Our Families

Praying and fasting can help us strengthen ourselves and our families. Our prayers for guidance are made more powerful because fasting emphasizes the earnestness of our prayers. Furthermore, when we fast and pray, we turn away from the things of the world and recognize our dependence on the Lord. In this way, we open our hearts to learn and accept God's will for us and our families.

Prayer and fasting also increase our ability to use the priesthood effectively. Both we and others are blessed when we learn that the power of the priesthood can be used only when we live the principles of righteousness. (See D&C 121:34–36.)

- Show visual 31-a, "Fasting and praying can help a priesthood holder administer to the sick more effectively."

The following story tells how one priesthood bearer learned the power of fasting and praying in helping him use the priesthood:

When John and Bonnie's small son became critically ill, the doctors diagnosed the illness as spinal meningitis. They told the parents that their boy would either die or be physically and mentally handicapped. As a bearer of the Melchizedek Priesthood, John decided to give his son a blessing. As he prepared to seal the anointing, however, he realized he did not know the Lord's will for his son. And so he simply blessed the boy that he would be comfortable.

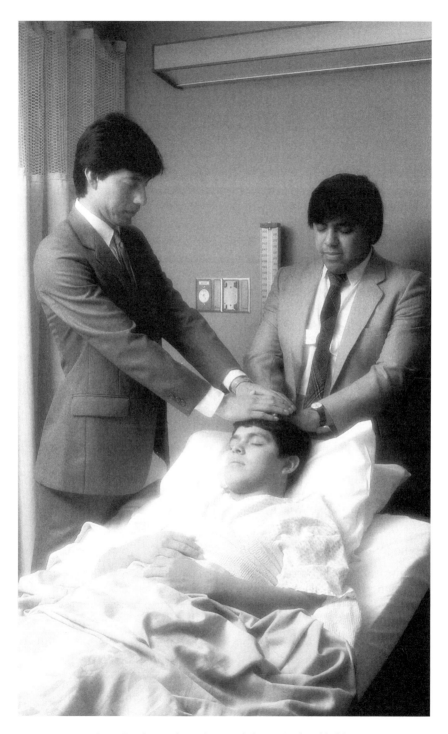

*31-a, Fasting and praying can help a priesthood holder administer to the sick more effectively.*

After the blessing, John and Bonnie began to fast to know the will of the Lord and to be able to accept it. At the end of their fast, John and Bonnie felt ready to accept the Lord's will. John again blessed his son. This time the Spirit whispered to him to bless the child that he would be healed completely. Their son was healed, and three days later they took him home from the hospital.

- How would their fasting have helped John and Bonnie if the answer to their prayers had been different?

### Teaching and Strengthening Our Families through Praying and Fasting

As parents, we should always pray to know the needs of our children and how to meet those needs. When one of our children is facing a particular challenge, for example, we can mention him or her in our family prayers. We should be careful, however, to always do this in a positive way. One father prayed for his son in these words: "[Heavenly] Father, we know that John is making a real effort to control his temper. We are grateful to see him growing and for thy help and support of our son. Please continue to bless him, and to bless us that we might not provoke him to anger but instead express our love and willingness to help him" (Marian P. Sorensen, "Teaching Children through Prayer," *Ensign,* May 1973, 34).

- How would this kind of prayer help a young man to overcome his problem?

Elder M. Russell Ballard told of an experience with his five-year-old son, who was afraid to start school. Recognizing that his son was afraid, he said: "Craig, you have a friend that will always be with you. Let's kneel down together and ask Him to help you" (in Conference Report, Oct. 1976, 129–30; or *Ensign,* Nov. 1976, 87–88).

Fasting and praying as a family can bring us great strength and unity, as the following story illustrates:

Alan was a young man who had received a call to serve the Lord on a foreign mission. He was anxious to serve, but as he began to study the language, he became very concerned because he was not able to learn it.

When Alan's father learned of his son's problem, he called his family together. He asked them to fast and pray that Alan could overcome his problem and serve a successful mission.

- How could such an experience strengthen our children? How can fasting and praying together unite families? Read 3 Nephi 18:21.

**Accomplishing the Lord's Work through Fasting and Praying**

A certain man came to Jesus, knelt before Him, and said:

"Lord, have mercy on my son: for he is lunatick, and sore vexed: for ofttimes he falleth into the fire, and oft into the water.

"And I brought him to thy disciples, and they could not cure him."

The Lord immediately cast out the devil from the boy. The disciples came to Jesus and asked, "Why could not we cast him out?" Jesus told them it was because of their unbelief, and then added, "Howbeit this kind goeth not out but by prayer and fasting." (See Matthew 17:14–21.)

In the following story Elder Matthew Cowley told of a bishop who understood the necessity of fasting and praying:

"[A wealthy young bishop in Honolulu] was called one day from the Queen's Hospital to come and bless a boy who had polio. A native sister had called him. He was her bishop, and she said, 'Bishop, come up here, my boy is stricken with polio, and I want you to come up here and administer to him and bless him.' All day she waited for him, and the bishop never showed up. All night he never showed up, the next morning he never showed up, but early in the afternoon here he came. She turned loose on him. She called him everything she could think of. 'You, my bishop, I call you and tell you my boy is here stricken with polio. And you your own boss, you have your cars; you have a beautiful yacht; you have everything you want; and your time is your own; and you don't show up. You just come now after a whole day.' After she had finished and couldn't think of anything more to call him, he smiled and said, 'Well, after I hung up the receiver yesterday, I started to fast, and I've been fasting and praying for twenty-four hours. I'm ready now to bless your boy.' At five o'clock that evening the boy was released from the hospital entirely cured of his polio. . . . 'This kind goeth not out but by prayer and fasting.'

"Now I doubt very much if he had gone up there the day before that would have happened. I think that prayer and that fasting were needed. So I think that we who hold this priesthood sometimes don't exercise it enough. You have to keep in condition, you have to keep in training with this priesthood which we have, then we'd always be prepared when we go out to officiate in the offices of the priesthood to give blessings" (*Matthew Cowley Speaks* [1954], 150).

It is not always necessary to wait that long before administering to the sick, but we should always seek to receive inspiration from the Lord before performing any priesthood ordinance.

- Why is it important for us to be spiritually prepared when we perform priesthood ordinances?

Just as priesthood bearers need to prepare to perform ordinances, those asking for blessings should also prepare themselves and their families to receive the ordinances. Elder Matthew Cowley told how a child's parents used fasting and prayer to prepare themselves and their child for a blessing.

"A little over a year ago a couple came into my office carrying a little boy. The father said to me, 'My wife and I have been fasting for two days, and we've brought our little boy up for a blessing. You are the one we've been sent to.'

"I said, 'What's the matter with him?'

"They said he was born blind, deaf and dumb, no coordination of his muscles, couldn't even crawl at the age of five years. I said to myself, this is it. 'This kind cometh not out save by fasting and by prayer.' I had implicit faith in the fasting and the prayers of those parents. I blessed that child, and a few weeks later I received a letter: 'Brother Cowley, we wish you could see our little boy now. He's crawling. When we throw a ball across the floor he races after it on his hands and knees. He can see. When we clap our hands over his head he jumps. He can hear.' Medical science had laid the burden down. God had taken over" (Matthew Cowley, *Miracles,* Brigham Young University Speeches of the Year [18 Feb. 1953], 8).

Many missionaries have discovered the blessings that come from fasting and praying. President Ezra Taft Benson told of an experience he had as a missionary fasting and praying with his companion:

"Out of personal experience, I know the efficacy and power of prayer. When I was a young missionary in Northern England in 1922, the opposition to the Church became very intense. The opposition became so strong that the mission president asked that we discontinue all street meetings, and in some cases tracting was discontinued.

"My companion and I had been invited to travel over to South Shields to speak in the sacrament meeting. In the invitation they said, 'We feel sure we can fill the little chapel. Many of the people over here do not believe the falsehoods printed about us. If you'll come, we're sure that we'll have a great meeting.' We accepted.

"We fasted and prayed sincerely and went to the meeting. My companion had planned to talk on the first principles. I had studied much in preparation for a talk on the apostasy. There was a wonderful spirit in the meeting. My companion spoke first and gave an inspirational message. I responded and talked with a freedom I had never experienced before in my life. When I sat down, I then realized that I had not mentioned the apostasy. I had talked on the Prophet Joseph Smith and borne my witness of his divine mission and to the truthfulness of the Book of Mormon. After the meeting had ended, several people came forward, some of them being nonmembers, and said, 'Tonight we received a witness that the gospel is true as you elders teach it. We are now ready for baptism.'

"This was an answer to our fasting and prayers, for we prayed to say only those things which would touch the hearts of the friends and investigators" (in Conference Report, Apr. 1977, 46; or *Ensign*, May 1977, 33–34).

### Conclusion

There are many other times when fasting and prayer can help us accomplish the Lord's work. For example, we can fast and pray for the families we home teach. We can also fast and pray as a quorum for one of our quorum members or his family.

Through prayer and fasting, we can be blessed physically and increase in faith and spiritual power. Such power is necessary if we are to be successful in our labors and in strengthening ourselves and others.

### Challenges

Determine some of the things you need to fast and pray about in your personal life and in your family. Think also about some of the needs of your fellow quorum members. Commit yourself to pray and fast for one of these purposes.

### Additional Scriptures

*Prayer*

- Matthew 6:5–15 (the Savior explains how we should pray)

- Luke 18:1–14 (we should be persistent in prayer)

- 2 Nephi 32:8–9 (we should pray before doing the Lord's work)

- Alma 34:17–28 (we should pray about everything we do)

- Moroni 10:3–5 (we can know the truth of all things through prayer)

- Doctrine and Covenants 19:28 (we should pray both in public and in private)

- Doctrine and Covenants 88:119 (we should establish a house of prayer and fasting)

*Fasting*

- Exodus 34:27–28 (Moses fasted before receiving revelation from God)

- Luke 2:36–37 (Anna served God by fasting and praying)

- Acts 13:2–3 (fasting can bring the inspiration of the Holy Ghost)

- Mosiah 27:23 (the fasting and prayer of others helped Alma recover)

- Alma 6:6 (the Nephites fasted and prayed for those who didn't know God)

- Alma 17:9 (missionaries fasted and prayed for the Spirit)

- Alma 45:1 (praying and fasting is one way to give thanks to God)

**Teacher Preparation**

Before presenting this lesson:

1. Read *Gospel Principles* chapter 8, "Praying to Our Heavenly Father." Assign a class member to give a three-minute review of that lesson.

2. Read *Gospel Principles* chapter 25, "Fasting." Assign a class member to give a three-minute review of that lesson.

3. Assign class members to present any stories, scriptures, or quotations you wish.

# REVERENCE

*Lesson 32*

---

The purpose of this lesson is to help us learn how to teach reverence to our families and improve our own reverence.

## Introduction

- Show visual 32-a, "Reverence in the chapel shows love and respect for God." Also, display the words of Leviticus 19:30 on a poster or refer to them on the chalkboard: *Ye shall keep my sabbaths, and reverence my sanctuary: I am the Lord.*

The following was written by President Spencer W. Kimball for Church members:

"We are a richly blessed people. The Lord has given us everything: the gospel of Jesus Christ, the light, the priesthood, the power, the promises, the covenants, the temples, our families, the truth. We should be the happiest people on earth. We should also be the most reverent people, but here I think every individual and every family should take a look at themselves. Are we a reverent people? Do our actions in the home and at church show reverence for our Creator?

"Sometimes we wonder. We attend sacrament meetings and conferences where children wander unrestrained in the aisles. During the service, we notice adults talking with their neighbors, people dozing, and young people gathering in the foyers. We see families coming late and filing noisily to their seats, and groups engaged in loud conversation in the chapel after the meeting.

"Our thoughts turn to investigators, friends, and those whose testimonies are fragile and developing. Are our meetings the powerful missionary tools they can be, where the Spirit of the Lord reigns and penetrates hearts? Or to sense the Spirit must we first block out many needless distractions?

"Let us examine reverence, not only its meaning and importance in the lives of Latter-day Saints, but some possible ways we can teach reverence to our children and improve our performance.

*32-a, Reverence in the chapel shows love and respect for God.*

**"The Meaning and Importance of Reverence**

"Reverence has been defined as a 'feeling or attitude of deep respect, love, and awe, as for something sacred.' To describe it as devotion to God is another way to express the meaning of reverence.

"Many of our leaders have expressed regard for reverence as one of the highest qualities of the soul, indicating it involves true faith in God and in his righteousness, high culture, and a love for the finer things in life.

**"Reverence for God**

"In modern revelation the Lord has helped us understand the meaning and importance of reverence.

"One such instance would seem to indicate that reverence toward the Father and the Son is an essential qualification or characteristic of those who attain the celestial kingdom. In section 76 of the Doctrine and Covenants, known as 'The Vision,' given to Joseph Smith and Sidney Rigdon in February 1832, we find:

" 'And thus we saw the glory of the celestial, which excels in all things—where God, even the Father, reigns upon his throne forever and ever;

" 'Before whose throne all things bow in humble reverence, and give him glory forever and ever.

" 'They who dwell in his presence are the church of the Firstborn; and they see as they are seen, and know as they are known, having received of his fulness and of his grace.

" 'And he makes them equal in power, and in might, and in dominion.' (D&C 76:92–95.)

**"Reverence for the Name of Deity**

"Another modern revelation directs us to hold in reverence even the very name of Deity; we are told not to profane the name of the Father, and even to avoid frequent use of it. (D&C 107:2–4.)

"Here we should remind ourselves that one of the Ten Commandments reads:

" 'Thou shalt not take the name of the Lord thy God in vain; for the Lord will not hold him guiltless that taketh his name in vain.' (Exodus 20:7.)

"It would appear that reverence for God and his name is one of the most important qualities we can develop" (*We Should Be a Reverent People* [pamphlet, 1976], 1–2).

- In what other ways can we show our reverence for God?

**"Reverence for the House of the Lord**

"In yet another area of extreme importance, the Lord has directed by modern revelation that we should have proper reverence for his holy house. In the important revelation given to Joseph Smith known as the dedicatory prayer for the Kirtland Temple, a directive was given that this, as with all other sacred temples erected unto the Lord, should be a place of reverence to Him. (See D&C 109:13, 16–21.)

"In a very real sense, what is said of the sacred temples of the Church is applicable to every 'house of the Lord,' whether it be a meetinghouse or any place where the Saints worship, or in fact, any Latter-day Saint home.

**"Reverence Involves Happiness**

"As with the other principles of the gospel, reverence leads to increased joy.

"We must remember that reverence is not a somber, temporary behavior that we adopt on Sunday. True reverence involves happiness, as well as love, respect, gratitude, and godly fear. It is a virtue that should be part of our way of life. In fact, Latter-day Saints should be the most reverent people in all the earth.

**"Reverence and the Home**

"Where, then, does reverence begin, and how can we develop it?

"The home is the key to reverence, as it is to every other godlike virtue.

"Let me emphasize the importance of teaching children to pray. It is during personal and family prayers that little ones learn to bow their heads, fold their arms, and close their eyes while our Father in heaven is being addressed. Behavior learned at home determines behavior in Church meetings. A child who has learned to pray at home soon understands that he must be quiet and still during prayers in worship services.

"Likewise, when family home evenings are part of home life, children know that there are special times, not only at church but at home, when we learn about our Heavenly Father and when everyone needs to be on his best behavior.

"Music is a special delight for children. Hymns that are frequently sung at church can become familiar in the home too. Small children especially could benefit if parents helped them learn simple hymns at home. In this way, children would eagerly anticipate singing at sacrament and other meetings" (*We Should Be a Reverent People* [pamphlet, 1976], 2–3).

▪ What ways have you found to improve reverence in your home?

**"Reverence at Church**

"Of course, parents should attend Sunday meetings with their children.

"The father and mother should work together to make sure that preparation for meetings is a pleasant family experience. The last minute rush to gather the children, dress, and hurry to meeting is destructive to reverence.

"When families fall into this pattern they are frequently late to church, there are often cross words and hurt feelings, and the children are often upset and restless during the service. How much more reverent is the family that prepares well ahead of time for meetings, that arrives at the chapel well before the meeting begins, and that sits together to listen to the prelude music and put worldly concerns out of their minds.

"Parents with small children sometimes have a difficult time helping their youngsters appreciate meetings and keeping them from creating disturbances. Perseverance, firmness, and preparation in the home are essential ingredients for success. If they are perplexed about how to handle their children at church, young parents might seek the advice of a more experienced couple in the ward.

"Often, before and after meetings, members of the Church cluster in the chapel to exchange greetings. Some seeming irreverence is due innocently to the fact that we are a friendly people and that the Sabbath is a convenient time to visit, to fellowship, and to meet new people. Parents should set an example for their families by doing their visiting in the foyers or other areas outside of the chapel before or after meetings. After a meeting, parents can help to carry the spirit of the service into the home by discussing at home a thought, a musical number, or some other positive aspect of the meeting with their children.

**"An Effort to Improve Reverence**

"We have discussed the importance of reverence and examined some of its meanings. We have also offered several suggestions about promoting reverence at home and at church. The real improvement in actions of the people, however, will come as local leaders and families combine their efforts to overcome their specific reverence problems. We envision an effort throughout the Church to improve reverence. . . .

"True reverence is a vital quality, but one that is fast disappearing in the world as the forces of evil broaden their influences. We cannot fully comprehend the power for good we can wield if the millions of members of Christ's true church will serve as models of reverent behavior. We cannot imagine the many additional numbers of lives we could touch. Perhaps even more important, we cannot foresee the great spiritual impact on our own families if we become the reverent people we know we should be. That we might work to develop greater reverence in our lives is my prayer" (*We Should Be a Reverent People* [pamphlet, 1976], 3–4).

▪ How can parents help their children enjoy church meetings and be more reverent? After class members have responded, have someone read the following suggestions:

**"Suggestions to Parents on Teaching Reverence**

"Parents can help their children enjoy church meetings by—

"1. Participating in Sunday School and sacrament meetings with their children.

"2. Making preparation for meetings pleasant and unhurried.

"3. Arriving five to ten minutes before the meeting is scheduled to begin.

"4. Sitting together as a family.

"5. Discussing a talk, message, musical number, or other aspect of the meeting afterward" (Spencer W. Kimball, *We Should Be a Reverent People* [pamphlet, 1976], 4).

▪ How can we teach reverence to small children? After class members have responded, have someone read the following suggestions:

"Parents with small children should try to—

"1. Help children understand what is happening.

"Young children may be able to occupy themselves quietly with a coloring book or workbook, but it is important to help them understand as much as possible about the meeting. An occasional whispered comment to clarify ward business or the speaker's message may help the child to relate to what is happening. For example, the father could whisper, 'That is Gordy's daddy speaking now. He's talking about pioneers.'

"2. Emphasize the songs.

"Singing can be one of the most enjoyable parts of the meeting for children. Encourage a child's interest in hymns by singing simple hymns at home and by teaching them to the child. The ward music director may be able to furnish a list of hymns to be sung in future meetings.

"3. Reinforce etiquette learned at home, in Primary, and in Sunday School.

"Help children remember to fold their arms and bow their heads during prayers and to sit quietly during the sacrament. Children should understand that it is discourteous to play in the aisles or to walk in and out of the chapel during the meeting.

"4. Set the example.

"Set a good example by showing interest in the meeting, communicating only when necessary and only in whispers, and encouraging children to do likewise.

"5. Ensure that children are ready for meetings.

"Visits to the restroom and drinking fountain should take place before the meeting begins" (Spencer W. Kimball, *We Should Be a Reverent People* [pamphlet, 1976], 4–5).

### Conclusion

When we are reverent we show our love and respect for our Heavenly Father and His Son, Jesus Christ. As we develop an attitude of reverence we can experience greater joy in life and in the teachings of the gospel of Jesus Christ.

### Challenge

List the things you can do to become more reverent in your own life and to help others, especially your own family, become more reverent.

---

### Teacher Preparation

Before presenting this lesson:

1. Prepare the poster suggested in the lesson, or write the scripture on the chalkboard.

2. Assign class members to present any portions of the lesson that you wish.

# LOVE AND SERVICE

*Lesson 3 3*

The purpose of this lesson is to help us learn the importance of Christlike love and service.

### Introduction

- Show visual 33-a, "Christ is the great example of love."

Jesus Christ loves every person. His ability to love is perfect. So complete is His love that the scriptures tell us that He is love (see 1 John 4:7–12). Christ shows His love by the acts of service He has performed for mankind.

As priesthood holders, we have the responsibility to become like Christ. To do so, we must learn to love as He loves and serve as He serves. Bishop H. Burke Peterson taught that "in a world and society where Satan is launching his most vicious attacks ever on the children of men, we have no greater weapon than pure, unselfish, Christlike love" (in Conference Report, Apr. 1977, 103; or *Ensign,* May 1977, 69).

### We Are Commanded to Love

One day as Christ was teaching, one of the scribes asked Him, "Which is the first commandment of all?" Jesus answered: "Thou shalt love the Lord thy God with all thy heart, and with all thy soul, and with all thy mind, and with all thy strength: this is the first commandment.

"And the second is like, namely this, Thou shalt love thy neighbour as thyself. There is none other commandment greater than these" (see Mark 12:28–31).

- Why are these two commandments the greatest of all the commandments? (If we love God, we will strive to obey all of the commandments He has given. If we love others, we will treat them as the gospel teaches.)

The Savior spent much of His life teaching about love. Sometimes His gospel is called "the gospel of love." He taught that only when we love others are we His disciples (see John 13:35). He explained that we

244

*33-a, Christ is the great example of love.* (The Last Supper, *by Carl Bloch. Used by permission of the National Historic Museum at Frederiksborg in Hillerød.)*

should even love our enemies (see Matthew 5:43–44). Just a few hours before His Crucifixion, Jesus said, "A new commandment I give unto you, That ye love one another; as I have loved you, that ye also love one another" (John 13:34).

President N. Eldon Tanner, stressing the importance of the commandment to love, said, "The only slogan we need in order to be happy . . . is: Love Each Other—three simple words" (in Conference Report, Apr. 1967, 103; or *Improvement Era,* June 1967, 29).

### Charity, the Pure Love of Christ

▪ Have a class member read Moroni 7:45–47. What is charity?

Elder Mark E. Petersen explained that charity is "the pure love of Christ which helps us to love both God and our fellowmen" (in Conference Report, Apr. 1977, 111; or *Ensign,* May 1977, 75). The following story told by Elder Marion D. Hanks shows how a father taught his daughter to develop and show charity.

"I think of a choice lady born with a severely handicapped body. . . . [She] spoke of an incident of her childhood. Playmates had called her names that . . . caused her pain and tears. When she reached home her father held her in his lap in his big strong arms and wept with her as he explained that . . . [this experience] could make her life fruitful and happy. 'Sweetheart,' he said, 'what the children said about you is true, but it wasn't fair and it wasn't kind. You do have a hump on your back and some other serious problems. But that isn't your fault. It isn't your parents' fault or Heavenly Father's fault. . . . If all your life you will try to be more fair and more kind to others than some of them may sometimes be to you, then you will be happy, and your life will be full and useful' " (in Conference Report, Oct. 1976, 42; or *Ensign,* Nov. 1976, 32).

▪ What does this story suggest that each of us can do to become more charitable? Have a class member read 1 Corinthians 13:1–3. Why is it so important to have charity?

Elder Theodore M. Burton explained that "charity is . . . love so great that we are willing to give a part of ourselves to others. . . . It is easy to say, 'I love you.' But love should not only be declared; it should be proved by actions. Love, unless demonstrated, is only a crashing cymbal or a booming drum which deafens the ears and does not soothe the soul" ("If I Have Not Love—," *Instructor,* June 1970, 201).

▪ Invite class members to think of opportunities they have to show charity toward others.

Being charitable will help us live happy, useful lives. If we do not develop charity, we shall be "as dross, which the refiners do cast out, (it being of no worth) and is trodden under foot of men" (Alma 34:29).

## Christlike Service

Our love for our Heavenly Father and for His children is shown through our service to others. President Harold B. Lee said that one night he had what "must have been a vision" in which he was told, "If you want to love God, you have to learn to love and serve the people. That is the way to show your love for God" (*Stand Ye in Holy Places* [1974], 189).

Christlike service is service given sincerely and often without reward to anyone in need. It may be unasked for or unpleasant and require much effort on our part. It may be needed at a time when it is difficult for us to give it. But no matter how it is given, it is service given simply because we love our Heavenly Father and His children.

- Why should we give service? Whom can we serve?

We should serve all people as we can and as they are in need. But Elder Thomas S. Monson reminded us that some need our help more desperately than others: "The sick, the weary, the hungry, the cold, the injured, the lonely, the aged, the wanderer—all cry out for our help" (in Conference Report, Apr. 1977, 108; or *Ensign*, May 1977, 73). The following story shows how one young man learned the importance of service:

The bishop called Steve into his office for a talk following sacrament meeting. "Here it comes," thought Steve. "I'm going to be the new teachers quorum president. Wow, is the ward ever going to heap hand-shakes on me. Mom will be so proud!"

"Steve, we have an assignment for you," the bishop said. "This is a special 'good neighbor' assignment. We're concerned about Hasty McFarlan. He needs someone to befriend him. He's not a member of the Church, but God's love reaches to all people, and we have the privilege of showing that love."

Steve was stunned. His mind raced back two weeks to when he and his friends had made fun of the old man by singing jingles and shouting jokes to him that they had made up about him. Disappointed and feeling guilty, he heard the bishop say, "I would like you to go out and visit him two or three times a week. Now if this assignment will be too much for you to handle, don't be afraid to say so."

Steve sighed and told the bishop he would do it. The bishop instructed him further regarding the assignment. "You can chop wood for the fire and get him food, blankets—whatever he needs to help him feel wanted. Be a friend. Your father is aware of the assignment, and he told me he would help you. Your Heavenly Father will be helping you too."

At age 15, Steve could think of things he would rather do—play foot-ball, hunt, fish, or play with his friends. But he knew he had agreed to the assignment.

Hasty lived a hermit's life in a little log cabin just outside of town. Once a year he had a free bath at the hotel, compliments of the sheriff. He wore a black eye patch and had a growth on the side of his head. Most of the kids and even some adults had the habit of making unkind remarks about him.

Steve arrived at Hasty's cabin very frightened. He knocked on the door but received no answer. Finally, after calling to the old man, he decided to push open the door. It was cold and dark in Hasty's cabin. He saw Hasty sitting on a soiled and mildewed blanket on his bed.

"Hasty, can I do anything for you?" Steve blurted out. He told the old man his name and that the bishop of the LDS Church had sent him. The old man said nothing, just stared at the floor. Steve left the cabin to chop some wood. He wondered with every strike of the ax why he was there. "Quit grumbling," a voice within him said. "The old man is cold and needs help."

Steve built a fire and tried to talk to Hasty, who made no response. He decided Hasty wasn't listening, so he told him he would come back the next day with a warm clean blanket. He was back the next day with a new blanket, as he had promised. Every other day for the next four weeks he visited Hasty. Finally, the old man began to talk to him. One day he said, "Boy, why do you come? I'm sure a kid your age could find better things to do than visit a sick old varmint like me." And then he smiled.

At Thanksgiving, Steve invited him to dinner. He did not come, but Steve's family took part of their dinner to him. There were tears in Hasty's eyes as he tried to thank them.

In time, Steve learned about Hasty's life as a sheepherder. He learned that his wife and children had died from a terrible fever and that a disease had robbed Hasty of one of his eyes. Somehow the old hermit did not seem ugly any more, and Steve hurried there after school to help him and hear his stories.

When Christmas came, Steve's family invited Hasty to dinner again. This time he came—clean, in a suit, and looking handsome. After din-ner the old man expressed his gratitude for Steve and his family. He said that his life had been a shambles, but the love they had shown him was making him a different person. Steve looked at Hasty and saw how happy he was; and inside, he felt his heart begin to grow warm. (See Terry Dale, "Hasty," *New Era*, Nov. 1974, 48–49.)

- How was the young man blessed by the service he gave? How has the Lord blessed you and your family as you have served others?

When we were baptized, we promised the Lord to "bear one another's burdens, . . . mourn with those that mourn; . . . and comfort those that stand in need of comfort" (Mosiah 18:8–9). We have the responsibility to seek out those who are in need. Then we have the responsibility to help them in love and kindness without being urged or commanded (see D&C 58:26–29).

## Conclusion

Bishop H. Burke Peterson reminded us: "The Master gave the commandment to all—not to a few in one land or a handful in another, not just to a family here or there, but to all his children, everywhere. Express love now! Show it now" (in Conference Report, Apr. 1977, 103; or *Ensign,* May 1977, 69).

President David O. McKay taught: "We have greater responsibilities than ever before to make our homes such as will radiate to our neighbors harmony, love, community duties, loyalty. Let our neighbors see it and hear it. . . .

"God help us as members of the priesthood, as members of the Church, to radiate . . . Love, . . . Charity, . . . and Service!" (David O. McKay, "Radiation of the Individual," *Instructor,* Oct. 1964, 374).

## Challenges

Pray humbly and sincerely for the ability to love as Christ loves.

Show love for your family by doing a kind act for each family member.

Show your love for someone in need by doing something kind for him or her.

Help your priesthood quorum plan a service activity.

## Additional Scriptures

- Matthew 25:31–46 (we serve God by serving our fellowmen)

- 1 Corinthians 13 (charity is the greatest attribute of godliness)

- Moroni 7:45–48 (charity is the pure love of Christ and a gift from God)

## Teacher Preparation

Before presenting this lesson:

1. Read *Gospel Principles* chapters 28, "Service," and 30, "Charity."

2. Assign class members to present any stories, scriptures, or quotations you wish.

# MORAL CLEANLINESS

*Lesson 34*

---

The purpose of this lesson is to help us understand the importance of being morally clean.

### Introduction

In today's world there are many different standards of morality. These standards often change with time and circumstances. By contrast, God's standards of moral cleanliness never change, for He is the same yesterday, today, and forever.

The scriptures tell us that "no unclean thing can dwell with God" (1 Nephi 10:21). The Apostle Paul wrote:

"Know ye not that ye are the temple of God, and that the Spirit of God dwelleth in you?

"If any man defile the temple of God, him shall God destroy; for the temple of God is holy, which temple ye are" (1 Corinthians 3:16–17). Our bodies are sacred. The Lord has given us bodies for a divine purpose, and He expects us to keep them clean and worthy to receive His Spirit.

### The Power to Create Life Is Sacred

It is important for us as holders of the priesthood to keep ourselves morally clean, for the blessings which are most important to us are linked to our moral cleanliness. One of God's many powers is the power to give life. He has shared with us His power to create life by allowing us to bring children into the world. Because this is a divine power, He has commanded all of His children to use it correctly and reserve it only for marriage. He has also told us that the desire behind this great power must be controlled and used within the bounds He has set. Elder Boyd K. Packer taught, "Much of the happiness that may come to us in this life will depend on how [we] use this sacred power of creation" (see "Why Stay Morally Clean," *New Era*, July 1972, 4–6).

Elder Richard G. Scott taught:

"Within the enduring covenant of marriage, the Lord permits husband and wife the expression of the sacred procreative powers in all their loveliness and beauty within the bounds He has set. One purpose of this private, sacred, intimate experience is to provide the physical bodies for the spirits Father in Heaven wants to experience mortality. Another reason for these powerful and beautiful feelings of love is to bind husband and wife together in loyalty, fidelity, consideration of each other, and common purpose.

"However, those intimate acts are forbidden by the Lord outside the enduring commitment of marriage because they undermine His purposes. Within the sacred covenant of marriage, such relationships are according to His plan. When experienced any other way, they are against His will" (in Conference Report, Oct. 1994, 50; or *Ensign,* Nov. 1994, 38).

Moroni tells us that virtue is "most dear and precious above all things" (Moroni 9:9). We must keep ourselves morally clean so we can establish our own families in righteousness and live in peace and harmony.

### God's Law of Moral Cleanliness

God has never changed His laws and commandments concerning sexual sin, although man has tried to change them to suit his own pleasure. The law of chastity means that a man must not have intimate physical relations with anyone except his own wife. The Lord has commanded, "Thou shalt not commit adultery" (Exodus 20:14). The law of chastity is not limited to just adultery, however. It extends to all improper uses of the divine power of procreation. Among the other ways man misuses this sacred power are fornication (including living together without marriage), homosexuality, abortion, and masturbation.

Chastity also includes cleanliness in thought and modesty in dress. The scriptures tell us that our actions are the result of our thinking (see Proverbs 23:7). We must keep our thoughts virtuous and be modest in our dress, speech, and actions.

- Have the previously assigned class member tell the following story by President Kimball.

"Sin, like a journey, begins with the first step; and wisdom and experience teach that it is easier to resist the first temptation than later ones, when a pattern of transgression has begun to develop. This is demonstrated in the story of the lark. Sitting in the high branches of a tree safe from harm, he saw a traveler walking through the forest carrying a mysterious little black box. The lark flew down and perched on the traveler's shoulder. 'What do you have in the little black box?' he asked.

" 'Worms,' the traveler replied.

" 'Are they for sale?'

" 'Yes, and very cheaply, too. The price is only one feather for a worm.'

"The lark thought for a moment. 'I must have a million feathers. Surely, I'll never miss one of them. Here is an opportunity to get a good dinner for no work at all.' So he told the man he would buy one. He searched carefully under his wing for a tiny feather. He winced a bit as he pulled it out, but the size and quality of the worm made him quickly forget the pain. High up in the tree again he began to sing as beautifully as before.

"The next day he saw the same man and once again he exchanged a feather for a worm. What a wonderful, effortless way to get dinner!

"Each day thereafter the lark surrendered a feather, and each loss seemed to hurt less and less. In the beginning he had many feathers, but as the days passed he found it more difficult to fly. Finally, after the loss of one of his primary feathers, he could no longer reach the top of the tree, let alone fly up into the sky. In fact he could do no more than flutter a few feet in the air, and was forced to seek his food with the quarrelsome, bickering sparrows.

"The man with the worms came no more, for there were no feathers to pay for the meals. The lark no longer sang because he was so ashamed of his fallen state.

"This is how unworthy habits possess us—first painfully, then more easily, until at last we find ourselves stripped of all that lets us sing and soar. This is how freedom is lost. This is how we become enmeshed in sin" (*The Miracle of Forgiveness* [1969], 214–15).

Controlling our thoughts, dressing modestly, and obeying the commandments of our Heavenly Father are ways we can keep ourselves pure and develop worthy habits.

When Alma's son had committed fornication, Alma told him, "Know ye not, my son, that these things are an abomination in the sight of the Lord; yea, most abominable above all sins save it be the shedding of innocent blood or denying the Holy Ghost?" (Alma 39:5).

We need to know and understand clearly the seriousness of immorality. We must not only live clean lives ourselves, but must also teach and encourage moral cleanliness in others, especially our children.

- How can we teach our children to be morally clean?

## Priesthood Power in Moral Cleanliness

No one can transgress the laws of chastity and expect to find peace unless he sincerely repents of the sin. The Book of Mormon tells us that the Holy Ghost will not dwell in unclean tabernacles (see Helaman 4:24). And if we lose the power of the Holy Ghost, it is impossible for us to use the priesthood authority bestowed on us. The Lord said, "And let all things be done in cleanliness before me" (D&C 42:41). When we are morally clean, the Holy Ghost can work through us to help us exercise our priesthood power properly. In this way, the priesthood is a great protection against sin. As we use it righteously, we not only serve others effectively but also obtain power to turn away from temptation. Elder A. Theodore Tuttle gave an example of how unrighteousness prevents us from using our priesthood authority:

"A foolish young man had been interviewed for a mission," wrote Elder Tuttle, "and even though he was asked some very direct questions, he answered them with lies. . . . Then he went out and tried to teach the gospel. That, of course, was the final test, and the test in which he failed. The missionary found out he could not do missionary work without the Spirit of the Lord. . . . So this missionary had to repent and . . . set himself right with those who had interviewed him before the Spirit of the Lord would be with him" ("Men with a Message," address to Seminary and Institute faculty at Brigham Young University, 1958, 2).

President Spencer W. Kimball gave some counsel that could have been helpful to the missionary in the above story. He taught that "any dating or pairing off in social contacts should be postponed until at least the age of 16 or older, and even then there should be much judgment used in selections and in the seriousness. Young people should still limit the close contacts for several years, since the boy will be going on his mission when he is 19 years old" ("The Marriage Decision," *Ensign*, Feb. 1975, 4).

President Kimball also explained that "among the most common sexual sins our young people commit are necking and petting. Not only do these improper relations often lead to fornication . . . and abortions—all ugly sins—but in and of themselves they are pernicious evils, and it is often difficult for youth to distinguish where one ends and another begins" (*The Miracle of Forgiveness* [1969], 65).

- How would President Kimball's counsel have helped the young missionary?

Keeping ourselves chaste and virtuous allows the Lord to bless us with spiritual power. Sometimes, however, we make mistakes. If this has happened, we should talk to our branch president, bishop, or mission president about it. He will advise us and help us to repent.

The Lord is as anxious to forgive us when we confess our sins as He is to help us remain morally clean. He knows our weaknesses and will provide a way for us to resist temptation. (See 1 Corinthians 10:13.) As an added help, He has sent prophets to guide us and teach us how to live the standards He has given us.

If we do whatever is necessary to become morally clean before the Lord, we will be able to "stand with confidence—unafraid and unashamed and unembarrassed—in the presence of God. This is the promise held out to every virtuous man and woman" (Gordon B. Hinckley, in Conference Report, Oct. 1970, 66; or *Improvement Era*, Dec. 1970, 73).

- How does our example of moral cleanliness influence the attitudes of our children? What can we do to set the proper example?

As priesthood bearers, we cannot carry out spiritual duties unless we are morally clean. The best way to accomplish this is to keep our bodies and minds pure and remember the sacredness of the power of procreation. If we set an example of obedience to the moral laws, our children will learn the importance of moral cleanliness and strive to remain morally clean themselves.

### Conclusion

The Lord has given us commandments to make us happy. Whenever we obey a law of God, we receive a blessing; but whenever we break a law, we suffer the result of our action. Living morally clean lives can benefit us in many ways. A clean, moral life promotes happy homes and marriages. It keeps us from feeling distrust and remorse. It keeps us worthy to serve the Lord. It permits us to go to the temple. It allows us as priesthood bearers to exercise the priesthood effectively in behalf of others. Most important, it helps us be worthy to dwell in Heavenly Father's presence throughout all eternity.

### Challenges

Take the necessary steps to be morally clean.

Discuss with your family the importance of moral cleanliness and how to be morally clean.

### Additional Scriptures

- Matthew 5:27–28 (we should not commit adultery in our hearts)
- 1 Timothy 2:9–10 (the importance of modesty)
- 2 Nephi 9:36, 39 (the rewards of moral cleanliness; the punishments for immorality)
- Jacob 2:27–28 (the Lord delights in chastity)

- Doctrine and Covenants 42:22–24, 80–81 (the penalties of immorality)

- Doctrine and Covenants 88:86 (moral cleanliness preserves personal freedom)

**Teacher Preparation**

Before presenting this lesson:

1. Read *Gospel Principles* chapter 39, "The Law of Chastity."

2. Assign a class member to read or present the story told by President Kimball about the lark.

3. Assign class members to present any stories, scriptures, or quotations you wish.

# THE ETERNAL FAMILY

*Lesson 35*

---

The purpose of this lesson is to help us understand our responsibility for establishing eternal families.

## Introduction

Eternal marriage is a basic doctrine of the Church of Jesus Christ and a very important part of the Lord's plan for us. Without it we cannot be exalted in the celestial kingdom in eternity. President Joseph Fielding Smith wrote: "Marriage, as understood by Latter-day Saints, is [an everlasting] covenant. . . . *It is the foundation for eternal exaltation, for without it there could be no eternal progress in the kingdom of God*" (*Doctrines of Salvation,* comp. Bruce R. McConkie, 3 vols. [1954–56], 2:58).

President Spencer W. Kimball said: "Our Heavenly Father has a plan for man's growth from infancy to godhood. . . . He intended that all men should live worthy to [be married] for time and all eternity" ("The Lord's Plan for Men and Women," *Ensign,* Oct. 1975, 2, 4). Temple marriage is the beginning of an eternal family unit. As a couple married in the temple have children and keep the commandments, they create an eternal family that will bring them joy and happiness forever.

## Preparing to Become an Eternal Family

- Show visual 35-a, "Eternal families begin in the temple."

To Latter-day Saints, a temple is one of the most important places on earth. In a temple, ordinances are performed that make it possible for families to live together forever in the presence of God. As heads of our homes and as priesthood holders, we have the responsibility for leading our families toward exaltation. This means that we have the responsibility to prepare our families to attend the temple. Such preparation begins with ourselves as we strive to honor the priesthood and live clean lives.

When men and women marry in the temple, they are married for this life, and they are also sealed together forever. Thereafter, any children they have are "born in the covenant," or automatically sealed to them.

256

*35-a, Eternal families begin in the temple.*
*(St. George Utah Temple)*

When a couple is already legally married and goes to the temple to be sealed for eternity, the husband and wife are first sealed together, and then the children are sealed to their parents. After their sealing, children born to them are automatically sealed to them as a part of their eternal family.

Whether we are preparing to be married in the temple or preparing with our family to be sealed in the temple, we must prepare in the same ways. Our first step is to set the goal to go to the temple. We should discuss with our wife and children the things we need to do to get ready, and together set a date. We should write down this date, pray for the Lord's help in meeting this date, and then do all we can to prepare. Because the temple is such a sacred place, we must also prepare ourselves spiritually to enter it. In the temple, we make covenants of great spiritual importance, for we promise the Lord that we will keep all of His commandments and obey Him in every way. It is necessary, therefore, that we live righteously and seek to obtain the Spirit if we are to be prepared to make these covenants.

- What can we do to prepare ourselves spiritually to enter the temple? (List the responses on the chalkboard. Answers may include those shown below.)

  *Pray often and sincerely.*

  *Read the scriptures regularly.*

  *Be morally clean and pure.*

  *Be humble and repentant.*

  *Faithfully hold family home evening and family prayers.*

As we sincerely do our best to become spiritually prepared, we will receive help from the Holy Ghost.

- Share the following story with class members:

One woman told how her family built their happiness together as they prepared to be sealed in the temple:

"Even as a child, I could feel the anger, the heartache, the bitterness, when my parents argued. Often I would cry myself to sleep because I knew things weren't the way they should be.

"I could feel the difference in the homes of my friends where their families were united in the gospel. . . . [Thanks to the bishop and home teachers, things started to change.] The gospel slowly became part of our lives. . . . The arguments became fewer—much farther apart. . . . Our family felt the responsibility of living as we'd been taught, especially now that we had a goal to work for [the temple]. If harsh words were spoken in haste, we returned words of love, calmly and sincerely. . . . We felt the excitement of helping one another. Mother and Dad didn't always have to ask three or four times; chores were done quietly, quickly, and promptly. Love and a desire to help overpowered the former bitterness, pride, and constant quarreling among us.

"What made the difference? So many things. Perhaps it was the reality of long-awaited dreams coming true. As family prayers and family home evenings became part of our lives, we learned to know and love one another. The way we were living allowed our testimonies to grow—testimonies of family prayer, reading the scriptures, family home evening, attending church meetings. Our real testimony was of the principle of repentance. And we also knew that God lived. After a period of time and with this testimony and the assurance that we were worthy, we were ready to go to the temple of the Lord to be sealed as a family for time and all eternity. . . .

"As we stood at the temple gates, a lump filled my throat. There was a moment's hesitation—and then we entered. . . . An attendant came to take us to the sealing room. Mom and Dad were there, faces radiant, dressed in their temple clothes. We knelt around the altar holding hands. An attendant held the baby so that she, too, was part of the family circle.

"And then the words were spoken that united us as a family for time and all eternity.

"I know my parents love me, because they had me sealed to them for time and all eternity" (Brenda Bloxham, "My Parents Took Us to the Temple," *Ensign*, Aug. 1974, 61–62).

For some families, financial preparation is also an important part of getting ready to go to the temple. This may mean years of planning, saving, and working together. Many families have sacrificed everything they own to go to the temple. We need to remember that no amount of money is more valuable than our eternal family.

To meet the expenses of going to the temple, we need to find out how much it will cost to travel to and from the temple. We should also estimate other costs such as food and housing. When we figure out these amounts, we should then determine how much we can save each month. If we do this, we will eventually go to the temple. (See the testimony of Brother Vaha'i Tonga in lesson 21.) Whatever we need to do to prepare ourselves and our families to go to the temple, we should start now. The rewards far outweigh any time and expense it may take.

- Have the assigned class member who has been to the temple with his family tell of his preparation and experience.

Young people who are not yet married have been counseled often by the prophets to prepare for temple marriage. President Kimball said:

"Even though many young people do not at this time have temples in their own communities, there are generally temples within a reasonable distance. . . .

"It is our earnest hope that when you have done your proper courting, that you would . . . go to one of these nearest temples to be sealed for all eternity so that your children will be permanently yours and that you will be permanently their parents and so that it will be an eternal marriage" ("The Marriage Decision," *Ensign,* Feb. 1975, 4).

### Building an Eternal Family

■ Show visual 35-b, "Families sealed together in the temple have the promise that if they remain faithful, they will be together for eternity."

Marriage in the temple is just the beginning of an eternal family. In order to build a family relationship that will last forever, we must be faithful to the promises we make in the temple. We must also treat each other with kindness and love. We should strive to make our homes a bit of heaven on earth.

As fathers, we can do much to build eternal families. We must honor our priesthood and show Christlike love. If we do, we will be strengthened by the priesthood and will receive inward promptings from the Holy Ghost that will help us build eternal family units. Some of the things we can do to build eternal families are:

Call our families together daily to have family prayer.

Call on someone to ask a blessing on the food at meals.

Take our families to church.

Pay tithing and other offerings.

Be honest in everything we do.

Kneel in prayer often and ask the Lord to help us as we teach and love our wives and children.

Take every opportunity to teach our families the gospel, especially at family home evening.

As we bless our families in these ways, we will enjoy the happiness of being part of a family that is eternal.

Unmarried priesthood holders can also help their families to be happy and to live as eternal families. When we understand the Lord's plan for our families, we can see that the members of our families are the most

*35-b, Families sealed together in the temple have the promise that
if they remain faithful, they will be together for eternity.*

important people in our lives. We should treat them with love and kindness and do all that we can to encourage and strengthen them.

- If there are unmarried priesthood holders in your class, discuss ways they can prepare for marriage in the temple. Ask them to explain why eternal marriage is important to them. Discuss things they can do to make their families happy right now.

**Conclusion**

- Share the following story with class members:

A young man from Mexico told the following story about his aunt and uncle. It describes the joy that can come from family life based on temple marriage:

"My Uncle David and my Aunt Guadalupe . . . were always quarreling. Their home was a disaster, and their children were suffering from witnessing the fights every day. Finally, Aunt Guadalupe and the children left to stay with her parents.

"During this separation, Uncle David met the missionaries and was baptized several days later. His new understanding of the gospel made him realize that a family was an eternal unit. He sent the missionaries to his wife and children, but they refused to listen. [Finally] they accepted the gospel, joined the church, and began living together once more. However, the fights and quarreling continued as before.

"They discussed the importance of temple marriage, but economic problems and constant bickering kept them from their goal. [But after much sacrifice and help from others they were finally able to go to the temple.] My aunt and uncle were sealed together with some of their children, and returned to Mexico with only 15 pesos . . . and no work for my uncle.

"Being married in the temple didn't erase these problems, but it did give my aunt and uncle strength to go on, even without money, and still feel happy.

"Little by little they found enough to eat, and my uncle was able to find work.

"I could see the great change on their faces and in their lives. They were happier than ever before, but my greatest surprise was that I never heard any more quarrels. In their place I heard words of love. . . .

"Recently, my uncle told me, 'Jorge, after being married for 24 years and suffering so much, we have found our happiness. It's just as if we were clean young people who just got married for the first time and who are now enjoying our eternal honeymoon' " (Jorge Carlos Tejeda Peraza, "Eternal Honeymoon," *Ensign,* Aug. 1974, 62–63).

We can receive great joy because of our eternal family relationships. Trials and hardships become easier when we share them with our families. Our lives become richer and more enjoyable because of the love we share. And we feel a great peace and comfort because we have the assurance that we can be together forever.

## Challenges

If you have not been married in the temple, make a plan and begin your preparation to be sealed in the temple with your family. If possible, get a picture of the temple and place it in your home where it can be easily seen. Below the picture of the temple, write the date your family has selected as a goal.

If you have been married in the temple, consider the things you must do in order to live with your family forever. Select one way your family can improve, and begin this week to work on it.

## Additional Scriptures

- Doctrine and Covenants 131:1–4 (we must be sealed in marriage to enter the highest degree of the celestial kingdom)

- Doctrine and Covenants 132:19, 55 (the blessings promised to those who are sealed together as eternal families)

---

## Teacher Preparation

Before presenting this lesson:

1. Read *Gospel Principles* chapter 36, "The Family Can Be Eternal."

2. Assign a member of the quorum who has been to the temple with his family to tell of his preparation and experience.

3. Assign class members to present any stories, scriptures, or quotations you wish.

# INDEX

# PICTURE SECTION

This section contains selected pictures from the Gospel Art Picture Kit (34730). These pictures can be used as an additional resource for gospel study and teaching at church and in the home.

## Old Testament

1.  Noah and the Ark with Animals
    *Genesis 6:12–21; 7:2–3, 8–9, 11; 8*

2.  Daniel in the Lions' Den
    *Daniel 6*

3.  Daniel Interprets Nebuchadnezzar's Dream
    *Daniel 1:7; 2*

4.  Jacob Blessing His Sons
    *Genesis 22:17–18; 26:4; 28:3; 48:21; 49; 2 Nephi 3:5; Jacob 2:25*

## New Testament

5.  Jesus the Christ
    *John 14:16–18, 26–27*

6.  The Birth of Jesus (by Carl Bloch. Used by permission of the National Historic Museum at Frederiksborg in Hillerød.)
    *Luke 2:1–16*

7.  Childhood of Jesus Christ
    *Matthew 13:55–56; Luke 2:41–52; Joseph Smith Translation, Matthew 3:24–25*

8.  Triumphal Entry
    *Matthew 21:1–11; Mark 11:1–11; Luke 19:29–38; John 12:12–15*

9.  The Second Coming
    *Malachi 4:1; Matthew 24:30, 36; Acts 1:11; Doctrine and Covenants 5:19; 29:11, 13; 88:96–97; 133:10, 20, 25, 48–49*

## Book of Mormon

10. Nephi Subdues His Rebellious Brothers
    *1 Nephi 17*

11. Conversion of Alma the Younger
    *Mosiah 27*

12. Captain Moroni Raises the Title of Liberty
    *Alma 45:24; 46:1–37*

13. Mormon Abridging the Plates
    *Words of Mormon 1*

**Church History**

14. Moroni Appears to Joseph Smith in His Room
    *Joseph Smith—History 1:27–47*

15. The Prophet Joseph Smith
    *Doctrine and Covenants 76:22–24; 135:3; Joseph Smith—History 1:25*

**Temple Pictures**

16. Salt Lake Temple
    Baptismal Font, St. Louis Missouri Temple

3

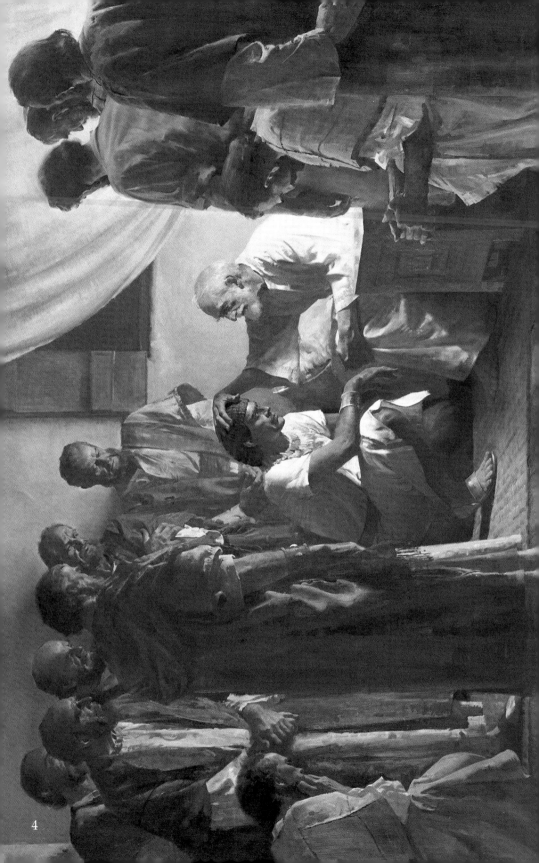

A.FRIBERG

15